T0290399

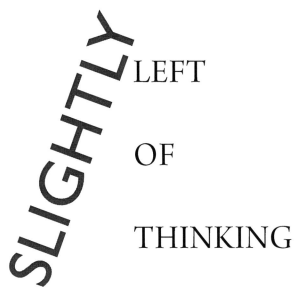

SLIGHTLY LEFT OF THINKING

poems
texts and
post-cognitions

Steve McCaffery

chax press   tucson   2008

Published by Chax Press
650 East Ninth Street
Tucson Arizona 85705

ISBN 978-0925904-71-3

Acknowledgments:
An earlier version of "Poetry in the Pissoir" appeared as a chapbook
from House Press, Calgary. An earlier version of "Opposite Poems"
appeared in *W* Magazine.

for Karen

"do not lean on the corridor of thought"
— *Fernando Pessoa*

Contents

Ars Poetica 5

Poems?

or minotaur catastrophes of concrete objects
in a paper domain?

What's that other word for silence?

The analogical opera?

The little object   *b*
before aporia kills it?

Slightly Left of Thinking

                         It passed / past
not a place though similar
cut out from   the inside cut
       up passed / past   point
tension
passed / past
Lascaux   towards   Duchamp
an immense extent-event
entelechy my mother called it
called   inasmuch   as
            calling completed it
passed history
past   progress
thought through
     to its end

in another start, another *polis* for sure
another end withdrawn from
                 accordance with
                 conclusion too brief, too sudden
to be brief
                 it said
"a finite finishing a final infinity"

just one.
just one more time

entelechy then *eidos*
a statue of Aquinas as Mercury

goddess of negativity,   a foot
touching the faculties   too late
again
too little the eye too
personal   passed / past it at
a wall

to wait on or weigh in
the three

passengers bald to
a pigment
a throat to it to

another generic
would it thus

wholly come
to the places in place of

an un-knotted thread   ?

stuck   in the sense of it
      feels to be sensing

     the non-space in
the opposite of art
too local for somewhere
behind before
that far, one says

that separate time

a little too early for
satisfaction

obstinate trace to put
passing
              passed / past
as if risk was
the rule
              of a difference made
              clear makes
permanent time for

the cut across cut in
the sense is as sense was

all at once
              all to where

the spiral returns
turns
       finished, a one
an end to it

word as is word becomes
passed / past
                     the same as
a year ago
              identical day ago
a year before being

before
            lens is what lens was
before altering
strengthening

this thus as
that than

of a wall
of a single blow   hurled beyond

cynical / clinical
passed   /   past
one asks,

who forgot it, otherwise, almost
a when or if why
a sample in smoke-effect

that
almost nothing
then

gone from then
come to us.

Tyrolian Night

Characters:
( ) = O
" " = X

The machine looks conservative but gosh what a leader in experimental phonetics!

(Firdausi thought it the new *hilaritas* when he changed his name to Basho.)

Tall frogs sit on a nunuphar built by lunatics and here is the room where the mirror-playing instrument occasionally interacts with the one who writes.

"So little to remember of the years before this happened."

Periplus to a plenum but with the intellectual activity of three, not as love in the middle, but on the side of godhead approaching *in absentia* the good things of will.

(As trade so ethics.)

But here, the symbol is adequate to announce proportionality to all attending.

Concealment quickly follows Lenin lodged in the Austrian Tyrol the night it snowed in Saskatoon with nuns swarming the Vatican.

Diapason the duration of its verbal components returning each night at eleven-o-three to a thin mist over many of the earlier objectives.

Along the seacoast a temporary five-year plan versus the bruised quintessence of a Nautilus.

"It could be good to go to a play instead of staying at home and reading James Essex's *Observations on the Origin and Antiquity of round Churches; and of the Round Church at Cambridge in Particular*, small quarto, 1782" when suddenly a hand appears to offer economic paradise.

The shell takes it and offers in exchange a highly innovative social history of sneezing.

Since then the burger master orders an effective system for annual economic exploitation.

"This could be wartime as once more the birds in excess of their feathers sing out proper names."

(Yours among them.)

Thinking this way creates a haunt for bohemians of an open market with its central violin explained by the fact that the man in tweed comes from Thessaly.

The petite DNA in the circular microchondria is not innate but certainly inventive in its senseless torment of the poor longshoremen.

"Let's take our next vacation in a big popular majority adjacent to the federal government building and whistle multi-corporate features as we go along."

The tiles are dark and unsophisticated in that region but each week summer returns as if the sun once shone.

Serfs rise to a rendition of addenda torn out of the final signature of Jean Francois Paul de Gondi's *Mémoires du Cardinal de Retz, de Guy Joli et de la Duchess de Nemours Nouvelle Edition* with provincial imprint fresh upon its scales.

"This brings us to a simply prodigious achievement despite the continuously successful call of an unknown requisition."

Something becomes language as the light goes out and the scientific consequence within the nature of receptacles stands finally for the source of all our spheres.

"It's been doing this for centuries while you were staying in the village of Erbach on the Odenwald living as a modernist from Milano sporting the word *chryselephantine* in your button-hole waiting to meet Phillip Whalen in the Preiss Hotel around the time Johann Philipp Ferdinand was born."

(But this shouldn't make you the multi-media pigeon voyeur that you want to be.)

The civil war has other effects as well as suddenness.

Starting with a prototype mistake it ends up in a practice of body fragments recollected among short-lived scenery in full flight.

(Other passengers lend money to off-shore steelyards taking two hours to lock up all the untenured faculty in the University of Geneva's Gynaecology department.)

At a rough estimate I'd say Medieval Greek doesn't have a precise term these days to describe a Futurist lexicographer.

"Why are the Alps called Catholic churches and filled with irksome vendors of second-hand sausage meat?"

Seems to me the name of a town on the west-bank of the Rhône would be equally appropriate given that the complete statement's still housed in a fire-proof structure made by the man who invented the Praetorian Guard.

"I feel I'm still trapped in the headquarters of some numerical system for Pythagorean locksmiths."

There's a chill to the night besides novel chocolate arpeggios clotting out the moon in a motionless communion some call Romanticism.

(The fact that I was writing this three days after the post office burned down is not retold in sagas from Iceland.)

There, the speaker adopts the persona of an aging Irish patriot named Desmond born out of the water in Machiavelli's abridged *History of Florence* by oxen connected to a different plot.

The insurgents assume names taken from the family of a species of Nymphalidae normally found in stagnant pools around Mount Rushmore and those ideas attributed to John Dewey transliterated from Russian into the argot of some late Constitutional Assembly.

"Pity the victims destroyed by all those Judeo-Hellenic Matisse programs."

"Hopefully it will rain for some of them at a Tang Dynasty bar mitzvah party as a man is acquitted of a crime he didn't expect."

But that night at the Safari World superstition conquered the security guards and caused a sectional detour between the giraffes.

A week later D'Annunzio finishes a play written entirely in the future tense.

Set in Shenshi Province, an abandoned child called Vishnu Rhizome sings an aria in two different but simultaneous voices.

(Outside it will have been snowing on Emmanuel Swedenborg as he completes his theosophic system in a small notebook purchased somewhere between Pennsylvania and Maryland.)

At which point a pejorative grief floods a film-script about a famous twentieth-century dictator known for his unrivalled Byzantine coin collection.

(The audience bicker over the pros and cons of Henri-Martin Barzun's theory of *simultanéisme* until the muffled footsteps grow louder.)

"It could be New York or *anno domini* but read the label carefully before going back on the ice."

Ingredients such as thistle and mildew delight in the thought of triple predestination brought on by covert Neoplatonic cartels after midnight in the era of mechanical respiration.

(The records of the Royal Academy guarantee a standard ethic to some human souls and seatbelts of a quality that will sustain their overuse if art persists.)

"But I was there when the letter bomb arrived back from historical oblivion then the next thing I know is I'm swimming in a pool of plain motif anticipating consequent morality."

However the goodness of delight in others still inaugurates a complex international problem.

"Then let's blast off the glass into the laws of habitat to pose ecological and predatory problems."

(It's what cougars do best.)

There are sometimes lips that never form a mouth across the scars and traces we call holocaust testimony.

"Perhaps memory converts them into meaning."

The flower's traces are still singable but not legible, except in the remainder with a "cunnynge" of Dominican origin.

(Then it happens again: a fifth-rate epilepsy oozes out of the word "rhapsodic.")

Crossing the Ganges reading Balzac doesn't get you to the tragic.

"Maudlin, granted, but the truly tragic is voiceless in Ann Bergren's account of the originary binding of women to writing."

Animal kingdom equals America however not too close to the White House.

"The trap of course presumes a loose enclosure for any missing or vagrant text such as Tiphaigne de la Roche's *Giphantia: or, A View of What has Passed in the World* the last two words of which are translated in the next line from Arabic when suddenly specific diversity restraint ratios are ruled a constant among the Maskes at Ludlow."

Intense ribbed patterning suggests the footnotes entered via a calcite soap solution.

Through an Arctic winter the leg-pendulum describes a greater arc, its vortex modified by fusel oil dropped from paraffin.

Form falls (for a time) into sentient amino-programmes following a statistical bridge connecting the few remaining Cartesian mind-grids working to monopolize known multiplicities in order to establish the birth of the thinking object.

(A co-ordinate range inaugurates the requisite Glossary of Greek fishes.)

Volatility Buddha architectures prove echo's the refusal to be twin.

"Don't worry, this facilitates panopticality as a cyclical non-numerical avenue to time."

Fanacalo esperanto down the cobalt mines gives way to knowledge that a library exists in which the front door's in the United States and all the books are in Canada.

"It's needless to add that the theological concept of a fall facilitates the origin of sexual difference and history."

(Pictorial structure from foreground to distance in a late work of Andrea Mantegna's produces tandem retinal repetitions, but a conflict emerges in the freedom = negativity equation.)

The problem pertaining to angelic annunciations is the echo options allowed the addressee.

"A practice of prayer has its hazards: wounds in water obvious to a thinker."

And here the spider silently expires, rectangular, in stories of unravelling where allegory passes into general semiosis.

A little later the car starts at the door to the room of the ideogram for "Grand Panorama" where someone has written out the Law of the Question as it occurs in Michael Daltons' *The Country Justice*, 1690, bound in full contemporary calf.

(Previously a neo-mannerist concept of discontinuous history guaranteed translated investment at a higher level of profit than simply "good.")

My name is Ben F, but not in this poem where the closest exit may be an entrance to the anechoic nerve bleep sutures.

"This is the place where solubility can happen as smectic marles collect in passing a coded potter's rule across a pebble powder to the waiting eyes."

Contiguous to a swan's death and at night with a weak demographic behind them demoiselle cranes fly over the Himalayas into their National Geographic dream.

A house decides to reverse its plan and become its own impossible event in current theories of the leisure class.

(Across the pain of a pin in the head the day has finally invented God.)

Instantly, as polymorph or gerund, a small mutant yeast colony cuts off the oxidative phosphorylation supplies destined for the Alte Pinakothek in Munich causing a lion hunt to start as oil on canvas.

"It is here that enthusiasm tends to generalize the tradition of tufted trees caught in the Gaspard Dughet landscapes popularized by the Chatelaine engravers."

The full moon rushes into rouge and precisely six years later a part of *L'Allegro* gets interpreted that escapes William Empson's comprehension in a Bangor toyshop.

(Elsewhere in the third-period of extra time a Scandinavian hockey player conceives a successful method of cloning a dog with a silent bark.)

Owing to the heavy rain each word means precisely what it signifies in *The Cottage Hymn-Book*, enlarged edition and suitable for both private worship and public use.

(But I wouldn't start a bar room quarrel over it, spell-check and the banks will do it for you.)

"We have a bibliography of worlds to read and H. von Pückler-Muskau's *Briefe eines Verstorbenen aus Frankreich*, Munich, 1830 is our guide!"

The Museum

The museum of promiscuity attempts to fold your skin into phonemic equivalence. Landscape here is a table sometimes filled with everything that's preconceptual. Imagine, for example, Groucho Marx as an ambiguity valve in all the recuperative possibilities of the multiple replicas of Andy Warhol's face staring at the contrary fascism of a binary bungalow regulation. New bacteria arrive by sea on square-base correlation questionnaires known as counterfeit substitutions, while back in metaphysics revolution reappears as the simulacrum's own revenge. It's always 4pm in this classic sector of disjunction, but after cross-dressing a tree to look like its park some exotic reciprocity at the MOMA takes the form of a twenty-first century thumbprint on a high-rise building soft as chocolate. All the barricades around incest form a subtle architectural disguise (the Brancacci Chapel, perhaps, where Christ raises Tabitha for sport). This *axis visualis* phase carries one to where Palestinians are caught in the repressive diffractions of a post-digitial "unhomeliness" program. Yet God still can't be equated with any convenient super-structural dominant. Is there still time, as a warm breeze enters the room where Bernard Tschumi thinks he's Hegel?

Per Verse

"Voluptuous" reads off classic "Volapuk." The arrangement of our myths as tiny six-legged exegeses in a stuttering closer to slides and caresses of the incommunicable than a tissue organon in arbitrary genus around some species named God.

Monotheism always implicates the polyvocal, it requires its apostles and saints, traits genetically linked to an undressed or undersized monad situated in the disintegrations of its numerous trace systems: sadomasochism, power, marginal theoretical works on the crucifixion before Pascal; its litany formulates as communal phrases: "have a nice cancer," "do you ever see smells," "does the mind divide into four epochs?" Chronotopes withdraw behind a static geometricality, the circle called "function," "the ellipsoids termed void." Quincunx and sycophant two simultaneities in intimacy, a modem of the new utopia and all the way out to a generic end.

Imagine God as anything other than an atheist. Perversion as the simple equation of "exigency" and "existence." What disintegrates requires the system it transgresses. A disposition to react beneath the level of the anaclitic propagation. Zucca working in the New Wave Cinema, or Diamant-Berger's 1921 version of *The Three Musketeers* form a vicious circle marking the casuist caught in complex molecular monstrosities. The libertine at a standstill waits for a footnote to simply happen in a text not written but yet read.

Neanderthal in seconds. The speech takes form as an aetiology of asceticism, a cave birth after the Christ-event, or was it earlier when sodomy emerged at Altamira in the south as a National Constitution of Ecstasy; obsessive depravity already composed. Disintegration of the entire sign system transcended by apathy in cold blood by the ebullition of a testicle close to a depraved tenderness. How to be an apostle of short-circuitries whenever a simulacrum of horror needs autonomous revulsion. Give it that and the saint emerges from the libertine, erect, tacit and unspeakable.

Flesh as speech is nothing but the carnal impact on biology with perhaps some evidence of violence in its micro-mismanagement. Obsessive depravity already composed, marking the legitimate hours as correlative with some visible condition (it is not "outside" nor "between" but a central rhythm in its myth, and surpassing its materiality). This self-reflexiveness permits the pharmakon to happen.

Synopsis

Truth is not a reclining nude as simple as Nietzsche descending
          a staircase.
Its form is curved, made
tangible the time Picasso was
sixty years before

anatomy.

Hamlet's Soliloquy

Something is happening to Denmark; a cockfight beneath a flower planted as a seed back in the era of complex engineering shifts it on its side. Will it come back in time to ease my subject position as a singularity? Venice is different. With its canals, small-scale profit incentives and French lexicographical lucidities it defines a rift between Catholic and Protestant marginalia that life in Elsinore never could.

In an age more erudite I would have written this differently. Denmark would have been divided into androgynous tables and diagrams and presented as a fashionable alternative to cartography. Fate would say the rest. The clock ticks its weight into space but is it a clock, or a group of soups discriminatingly sprinkled with salt and largesse from France? "Why is the sun at the bottom of the sea?" asks the infant materialist, cooking sauces as she would a theory of Rococo cosmetics. Piranesi has an answer in a form of drainage that leaves the mind unscathed in a pure equipoise. In his days purists swam in their own eschatologies as music undulated congruent to paradox. If the car won't start today will it finish tomorrow? Why state this in the form of a question? Think of Hogarth and the Sophists and what happened to interrogation back then. A clown in a marketplace might be that marketplace and pass unnoticed, but in a paradigm reality shift like mine it slips into a passing image catching the eye before it disappears into an echo of Quintilian the day he spoke of Denmark being Denmark.

A false map of any nervous system can just as easily be fabricated to look like a portrait of me or my autobiography in the way non-visual appearances can fool the mind into thinking I was Macbeth in another life. It can even be made to look like Denmark. A sun ascends spinning into textured light to be immediately eclipsed in a shower of ideology that soaks me to the skin. History was important then when the heroes of performativity in their superficial disguises tried to mesmerize each gathered crowd of simulacra. It was always the present then, but suddenly a dog barks ardently but not close enough in time for me to imitate. What's needed is a different map of all my possible transformations: Lord Byron on fire and little Gertrude in her scotch-plaid neuroses, twin phantoms of pliable filaments and both of them fluent in Esperanto. And everyone deposited before the Quadruped Goddess who brought us here in the first place. It started as a day and now it's an epoch. How things expand. Will it ever end as it pauses and passes through limitless space until crashing into some *ars combinatoria* of all that's infinitely possibly feminine?

A bird, a baluster, a vase, a hieroglyph for an armpit, a disconnected cylinder en route to Mars dragging a potent metaphor behind it. These are all indoor species of hyperbole carelessly distributed among "mists of desire," "elixirs of love," "bonnets of folly." The poet here paints but the painter paints a hitherto unnoticed connection between anatomy and architecture. Each wall has a corresponding masculinity or some similar skin disease. There are scar tissues repeated as vast formal ghettos over each façade, a heart pumps itself into a landscape that's being subdivided into hospitals, tonsils and jails. In recent times the difference between singularity and populace that made the canons of proportion so important has disappeared. An uncontrollable sprawl has entered the history plays and rendered Denmark less durably pleonastic. Numerous ubiquitous sites are springing up to return space to common air. All the sparrows are blind now but sing proportionately louder.

Eczema invades each futile move to a midsummer dream's nightmare forcing it back into pastoral and its generic problem of the one-dimensionality of ancient sheep and goats. It's hard to ontologize geography, convert Arcadia back to its idiot savagery, but Denmark is different, it still petitions the dream phase of a child born before its time. The flowers of its gentry might be Proclus, Leibniz, and Shaftesbury: if that way a certain optimism returns and sets the book back in its proper conceptual space, well done!

As I write this, or having written it, the thought of writing disappears and Denmark never happened.

Parmenides

Over here, or there, seems to be a potential for action, or then again, over here, or there, might be a different place mentioned in an alternative tour guide. An action includes a reason, a potentiality and a translation leading to fatigue, weight gain, and hot flashes. The voltage currently running through the pet canary named Logic is the same voltage running through the entire last century of existence named Post. This is where it left it exactly as they found it. This is where it should have been some time ago had it not interfered with it. It may be posited in language as position is or sometimes at least in a case where the yards and yards of string unravel in the word yard uttered by it, or through it, into the yard outside. It is fortunate that inside is not a possibility. Possibly, however, or, wherever it moves there is, in some way or some other way at this point a necessity to pause and cross between the Logic and the Post, both mentioned in the present reading which may, or may not, be interrupted by a thought upon the sophistication of current condominium living or dying. If that thought is, or is not, appropriate to the alternative text at hand, or not at hand, the voltage running through the pet canary named Logic may, or may not, interfere with the seven, or more than seven, current possibilities. What remains possible, or impossible, at this point is a renewed desire to intercept, or not intercept, the current voltage flowing into the sophistication of current condominium living or dying. At which point speech, or the thought of speech, may formulate an identical or different axiom, thereby permitting a quotation from Parmenides to enter the text with relevance or irrelevance.[1] What will be certain here, or somewhere else, is that a different frog named Cognitive will have plopped into a beachfront pool named

Infinity. It will then be coterminous with it if it aligns the axiom to a place beneath it or beyond it. The yard might then unravel into several, or more than several, subsets causing the voltage running through the pet canary named Logic to remain unaltered. This event may, or may not, occur within a space of History, or at the spot where the pet canary named Logic disappears, or reappears. The alternative tour guide might remain alternative but only to the point at which all current voltages are directed into the current Labor of the Negative. Here, it wishes to say it is not where it should be having been interfered by it before it entered the *conatus* of its being. The pet canary named Logic might now reflect upon the sophistication of its own condominium living or dying and yet remain on, or suddenly depart from, the same branch on the tree called Annihilation where the current voltage running through the different frog named Cognitive enters its very own new axiom. Exciting indeed! However, Manifestation may, or may not, adopt a viewpoint different from the one determined, or not determined, by the Beachfront Pool named Infinity. Only then will it position itself correctly, or incorrectly, in the space between it or before it. It will then be, or not be, its own simple fact that over here seems to be a potential for action. Yet an event caught in an act is not a situation, therefore the one is not [Plato, *Parmenides*]. Hence Logic emerges as the Cognitive Labor of the Negative intercepting the names of the pet canary and the different frog in the *conatus* of their being. What is now certain is that the different frog and the pet canary once named Logic are not a singular event caught in a singular act occurring in a space of History. This will have been true or untrue from the start if this is a text, or not a text, on love, nor a poem on meaning. At which point the current voltage might dissipate into several, or more than several, alternative possibilities: ancestral repetition, liberated continuities, Judith Butler on a warm

September night, the transparency of nitroglycerine.   Perhaps Judith Butler activates an incomplete "I" positioned between, or beyond, a different pet canary named Language caught up in the Labor of the Negative. At which point it will be, or not be, its very own and singular situation between or beyond it as it leaves the branch on the tree named Annihilation if this is the final chapter of a book entitled *The Conatus of Being*, conceived in the yards and yards of string unraveling in the word yard uttered by it or by Judith Butler standing in the yard outside.

1. "Thinking and Being are the same Thing."

'Pataphysical Poems

'Pataphysics:

"the ecology of hypothetical experience"
—Tom Conley, Introduction to Gilles Deleuze, *The Fold*

A BLANK WALL FOR MICHAEL TAUSSIG

it is the power of the copy to influence what it is a copy of it is the

Apologia pro vita sua

1

i am a page if i am not a page
i will be a page when i will not be a page
i want to be a page as i do not want to be a page
i have become a page but i have not become a page

2

i am a page if i am not
i will be a page when i will not be
i want to be a page as i do not want to be
i have become a page but i have not become

3

i have not become a page if i have been
i do not want to be a page when i do not want to be
i will not be a page as i will be
i am not a page but i am

4

i have not become the page i have become
i do not want to be the page i want to be
i will not be the page that i will be
i am not the page i am

Ghost Poems

Preface: A Metapoetic

Because I like the pronoun "we" I like to put the verb "to put"
between the first person pronoun "I" and the verb "to like" with
the definite article "the" placed before the word "poem."

Now we can correct some of the poem's mistakes.

It is not a sonnet
even though it rhymes sometimes.

The reference to Fra Angelico is incorrect
as is the spelling of "Tennison."

Three and a half inches by seven miles
is its correct measurement.

It has thirteen not fifteen verbs
and seventy-six not eleven

definite articles.
There are no gerunds

and only three proper names
if mine is put in brackets.

This first poem occupies a single page; there are twenty-eight lines, 119 words, 16 commas, 8 full stops, 2 sets of quotations enclosing 17 words, and 21 different alphabetic characters. It seems to be a parody of Cicero's presentation on Academic Skepticism, but it's only partly written in Latin. One line proposes clouds are actually contradictions of the sky and that good deeds are best explained against a background of evil. The poem's dominant sense is acoustic, closely followed by the olfactorial and visual. I'm uncertain why the reference to Aristophanes follows a brief allusion to the geometric probability that hens' eggs can be naturally geodesic, or why an unnamed subject tries to find two identical leaves in a forest before lunch in the Café Pyrenées. My favorite line is the eighth that ends with the word "indiscernible." My least favorite is the single line that reads "the square's two sides."

The second poem is written in *terza rima* and runs to thirteen stanzas. The first opens with the phrase "nothing fails to do justice to the cause of rats;" it contains seven references to other animals and to one insect (the common or garden *musca domestica*). All are listed as a catalog. Sixteen lines that use thirty two words deal with the possibility that Socrates was an alien space-time worm. This conceit occurs after a wonderful description of the Eleatic countryside and a reference to mating patterns in Megarian goats. The theme of the poem seems to be perdurability and the tendency for utilitarianism to collapse into a moral theory of sentiments. The switch from stanza one to stanza two is abrupt and ill managed. After the first stanza ends with the receding flight of a goldfinch, the second opens with the line "Our finite world is bitter sweet" and then moves into an apostrophe on Anaximander's discussion of the teleological implications of the uncaused cause. The laudation occupies the rest of the stanza and ends with a speculation on the destruction of world order in the event of a successful policy of conquest by "Cortes or his ilk." The conceit that a paradox is a buoyant self-refutation is delicately handled but the description of a student of Schopenhauer eating a state-subsidized pastrami sandwich as he reads a poem entitled "Ode to Perpetual Peace" fails to pull off the obviously humorous intention and the effect (if any) is utterly banal. Stanzas three to twelve are taken up with two convoluted and protracted debates on whether strictly philosophical problems can be resolved by consistent appeals to revealed religion, and whether same-sex "verbisophistry" was a common phenomenon in seventeenth-century Sweden. There is, however, one singularly brilliant simile "the fuzz grew on his existential beard like a comma in Hebrew." There is a well-handled digression describing two male tourists called Allen and Alan in a Moroccan bazaar. Allen is explaining to a local basket seller the difference between a coin and a pebble. His monolog ends with the enigmatic phrase "such a meal as this was meant for yesterday, how fortunate the future." The final stanza segues into a tedious reflection on creditor acquiescence in the afterlife, insisting that Heaven is a Bank and God never invests in his own creation, yet the ending is effective: "subtract the one that closed a sin."

The third poem is a *limérique* about a drug addict from Poland who over imbibes and tries to eat two figs while drinking a glass of sherry. The rhyme scheme is "Krakow" "smack off" "drink" "think" and "go whack off." Apart from the one proper name which is set in 12 point Caslon italic, the entire poem is printed in Frutiger sans serif. It occupies the top half of a single page (page 123) and immediately below it is a similar *limerique*. In fact, the entire book of 241 pages is filled with poems in this form. Many are witty, several humorous and some in extremely bad taste. The book, printed in Singapore, lacks both its covers and its title-page. There is an inscription on the half-title which reads "from Jack to Molly, all my best with a few suggestions for next week in the caravan."

The fourth poem is also a *limérique* but from a different book of entirely Irish verse. It tells the story of a person from Kent who has a crooked penis (presumably from birth) causing him severe complications during sexual intercourse. Although no specific sexual act is described it's clear that the author has little sympathy for the poor person's condition and concludes the poem in a terse, insensitive manner with the curious phrase "instead of coming he went."

The fifth poem is a *sonnette* in Petrarchian rhyme scheme, and written in Scottish dialect. It asks whether Pound's "Hugh Selwyn Mauberley" compares favorably with Hugh MacDiarmid's "Second Hymn to Lenin." My favorite passage is the one that ends with the phrase "an quentiss slycht him rycht and fycht" but the last line that starts with "Give fyff yet kynryk yhwman" fails to tie off the obvious geo-political sentiment.

The sixth poem, a *koncrete* poem by a well-known Bolivian philosopher, utilizes 79 French words arranged in the shape of the Eiffel Tower and deploys the letter "e" seven hundred and sixteen times. In addition there is a smaller grouping made up entirely of cedillas to form the charming shape of a Parisian pigeon flying directly into the tower. Collaged around it are numerous onomatopoeic words taken from children's comic cartoons. "Spashoom, queflunque, basheeeen" effectively balance the post-linear visuality of the collage constellation with an acoustic residuality that facilitates a synaesthetic reception of the entire piece. Unfortunately the page has been badly creased (probably bent over at some point) and an unpleasant diagonal cuts across the entire page sadly marring the beauty of the tower pattern.

The seventh poem declares itself to be a "Poster Poem." Its dimensions are fifteen feet wide and forty-six feet high. It consists of a single word "LIXIVITATE" in a Futura Condensed typeface. The ink is magenta on taupe hessian, the edges frayed and the entire surface generally dirty from frequent touching, but overall the piece is sturdy. It was first observed on July 23 flying from a flagpole in Trafalgar Square, London and then again, on August 3, 1963 from the side of an ocean liner. It is now displayed on the wall of a small gallery in Soho, New York.

The eighth poem is written in German but quotes two lines of Verlaine in French. The subject is architectural impermanence as reflected in some crumbling ruins on the outskirts of an unnamed village that the speaker claims he is visiting. Of the twelve stanzas that comprise the text five end with a question mark. There are fourteen proper names all but one being replaced by asterisks after the first letter. The poem leads me to infer that these are the names of contemporary architects whose arrogance shows in their recent designs. One design the poet mentions is of a hospital in the shape of three interconnected kidneys, another is a brothel in the shape of an erect penis with the testicles forming two adjacent rotunda. The opening description of sunrise is particularly powerful, with its terminal phrase *"der Herbsttag nun"* clearly borrowed from Hölderlin's *Mein Eigentum*. Despite the religious overtones permeating the poem, there is no explicit reference to Christianity or indeed to any other organized religion. There are three political references (to a current war, a corrupt minister, as well as financial mishandling of pension funds) and—curious in a German poem—a short description of the construction of Covent Garden Theatre in London. The concentration of subjunctive clauses toward the end, together with the general catabolic movement of the subject, lend to the piece a lingering melancholy, not unlike the one occasioned by Gray's *Elegy Written in a Country Churchyard*.

The ninth poem, although written in English, is an *elegie* on the death of a celebrated Dutch chocolate manufacturer. The disappointing brevity of the piece is amply compensated by its terse and pithy handling of stock conceits. The mixture of restrained rhetorical ornament and vernacular speech is managed with consummate grace, although the emphatic antitheses that populate the middle stanzas serve little beyond displaying sound effects. There is a dexterous allusion to Ciceronian concinnity in line twelve, crowned with a superb *figura sententiae* in the fifteenth. The short description of a dead man's coffin with its detailed portrayal of the carved handles remains a triumph in parabolic aphorism, negotiating the subject, the mood and consequent metaphysical reflection with consummate dexteritie. My favorite word in the poem is "pulchritude" (applied to the dead man's cat) and least favorite "graced" in the phrase "well graced in difference and prudence mild."

The tenth poem, extending to two manuscript volumes, seems prompted by a recent criticism of Aristotle. In its three thousand and odd stanzas it defends the Greek thinker on all counts: his rhetoric, his metaphysics, his gynecological treatise and his poetics. The poem is amplified by copious footnotes many of which extend into short prose treatises on such subjects as the proper form for political writing, the correct manner of eating runner beans and a lengthy castigation of contemporary mores, especially attendant on theatrical performances. The references to Wycherley, Congreve and Aphra Behn, together with the eighteen references to "pshytte" and six occurrences of the word "hornstrumpot" allow me to date the piece to the second half of the seventeenth-century which renders the anachronistic reference to a subway train and what can only be taken to be a cellular phone uncannily prescient. The poem's style seems adapted to a middle-class rather than aristocratic audience with much remonstration upon the habits and postulates of the Dewsbury sodomist and apostate John Perrot. The plenitude of Latin quotations weakens the overall power and surge of the poem's "national" rhetoric, with the ill-chosen passage from Seneca ("*venustissimae sunt periodi, quae fiunt vel ex antithesis*") effectively destroying what otherwise would have been a fine stanza on the overt turpitude of the Anglican Church. The bizarre clusters of Tahitian loan-words are surprising and the unpleasant abundance of consonant groupings tend to overcomplicate the phonematologization of the reference to Aristotle's theory of the temporal cleft.

The eleventh poem is a 24-line translation of the first ode of Anacreon. It was completed when the translator was a student at Trinity Kollege, Dublin. No doubt the provost would have commended the poem for a prize had he not doubted that the University would countenance anything so amatory and convivial. There are references to Baptista Porta, Philostratus, Basilius, Adamantius, Ben Jonson, Baxter and Longepierre in the one accompanying footnote. The poem occupies pages 37 to 40 in a book of small duodecimo format. The book's handsome contemporary binding of dark red morocco is especially pleasing with its covers richly gilt "aux petits feux," a gilt smiling infant Bacchus stamped within a central rhombus with fleur-de-lys and small dots at the outer corners, within a single fillet four-lobe shape, echoed by four decorations with tendrils, pointillé and tiny fleur-de-lys, and by six motifs mainly pointillé, surrounded by small dots, some with a tiny pointillé halo, with four fillets (two being pointillé) with inner corner-pieces including tendrils, vine leaves, grape clusters, pointillé and small crowned wine jugs. All of this is set within an outer decorative border with tiny linked fleur-de-lys. The spine has raised decorated bands in blind with rosettes pointillé and inner dentelles decorated in blind.

The twelfth poem is on the subject of fishes and fishing, drawing heavily on the *Alieuticon* of Oppian. There are seven morbid, opening stanzas dedicated to the self-manufacture of fish-hooks from fragments of lead coffins histrionically delivered by their vacating corpses. The poem subsequently stabilizes into factual accounts of the mating, breeding, and fighting of the various species. The description of the grey mullet's breeding haunts and of catching sturgeons by net and musical accompaniment is especially successful. A final stanza describing such fabulous aquatic creatures as the Triton and Nereid ends abruptly owing to the author's death at 7.36pm on August 11, 1827 at the age of nineteen.

The thirteenth poem is a narrative *pome* written in polter's measure and celebrates the legendary victory of Captain Sam "Cannonball" Smirke in a 1932 US National Snooker Championship. The poem is set in a bar room in Poughkeepsie and, after an initial invocation of the muse of sport, ("Come Heavenly Dame my drooping powers repair . . .") opens with a brief history of the game, then quickly enters into its main subject: the heated rivalry and close fought competition between Smirke and Kenny "off-the-cushion" Dahl. The mock-heroique tone is moderately effective (with billiard cues likened to "stiffened tendrils" and cue chalk to "sapphire sand"). However, the overuse of personification reduces the poem to self-parody. That said, there are marvelous ekphrastique portions, most memorable being the slow slide of the cue between Sam's left knuckle before he broke the pyramid to open the game and Kenny "off-the-cushion's" facial grimace as the black ball hovered at the edge of the pocket without dropping. There is a brief appearance in the poem (apparently based on facts) by both Wallace Stevens and Gertrude Stein, the latter cheering for Dahl and exhibiting facial grimaces of disbelief at his narrow and surprising defeat. Stylistically the poem is of great interest primarily for its use of a colorful version of Harlem Jive complete with such vivid phrases as "go dig that dicty fay he sure beat up the chops on dat dare cushion-kisser cat" and "thazza blip and hummer of a cue for this low frolic pad."

The final *pome* is a composition of my own written earlier this year in response to re-reading Chaucer's *Canterbury Tails* from a perversely *masculiniste* viewpoint. The poem is currently housed on the hard-drive of a Mac G 4 computer on the second floor of 104 Oakland Place, Buffalo, New York. It contains minor revisions and a significant expansion of three lines totaling 27 words of an earlier draft shown below:

The Husband of Bath

She never let me get a word in
      edgewise
vulgate, cadence, alliteration
    expedience for each amplified disappearance
into that spot the size of a shilling
across wuthering patristic lamentations
the lone
      and level sand
            stretched
                 far away

The Dangers of Poetry   for Italo Calvino

Maybe you don't like this poem or perhaps you don't want to read it perhaps you should do something else like wash last night's dishes or watch TV if I were you I'd try reading a good book or even start to write one but perhaps you haven't stopped reading this poem just yet while you're wondering what else you could read or perhaps your interest in this poem has miraculously changed maybe you're enjoying it or finding it a challenge or perhaps you're simply thinking it would be a waste of precious time having read it so far to not read it to the end or perhaps there's nothing you can do because perhaps this is a class assignment that you can't get out of or the start of a Conference on the Life and Work of Italo Calvino you've paid a lot of money to attend or perhaps it's a punishment prescribed in a maximum security prison you're now in for five or even ten years or perhaps reading this poem has induced paralysis and you can't move not even to blink your eyes or perhaps you believe it can't get worse but it does get worse and you think all these thoughts again and then compare this poem to the start of Italo Calvino's novel *If on a Winter's Night a Traveler* and that the two might be related perhaps you think that this poem was actually written by Calvino under the pseudonym of Steve McCaffery and then you think that this might be the poem Calvino didn't write but wished he had and by this time an entire week has passed and you're still at your desk at the office because you never went home and perhaps you couldn't have anyway because a friend called to tell you that your house burned down and all your pets and family were burned to death because you were still reading this poem.

47 S.L.O.T.

Design for a Walking Poem:
In Memoriam Jackson Mac Low

The sound of a praying mantis placed in Tibet is magnified and transmitted by satellite to stanza one where a computer program translates it into a series of graphic images. These images are passed into stanza two where they are instantly printed onto fabric that proceeds in a boustrophedon movement into stanza three. Here a laser scanner cuts the fabric into a predetermined shape and pattern from which numerous national garments are assembled. The stanza puts one of these on and walks purposefully into stanza four where a taxi eventually stops and takes the entire poem to an airport just in time to board a waiting plane to fly it somewhere other than Tibet.

Fifteen Designs for Eighty Street Corners and a Central Square

(Part I of Alphabet City)

L   F   E   W   A

V   I   K   L   M

N   T   X   Z   Y

O

That cosmological synthesis called breakfast, or: The Battle of Jena

"I" as a revelation empty of itself asserts that it's hungry and thinks

it wants to eat. It "is" but "it" doesn't exist. When meaning is subtracted from a non-A at the end of any alphabetical sequence it renders a zero point the impossible instant that's there, a something that must be in its non-being remembering the memory

it remembers. For example, I am becoming until I have become,

but what makes me say "I"? It is I, but it doesn't exist and I was

before I am becoming such that I as a word in the world

will not occur. But it does and it forgets itself and suddenly a

non-I is there and therefore a something, a desire without life in

a parenthesis around my I that will not occur. At this point it can't

say "I" in order to come back. But if I was a woman and a man was

a brick it could become a house that thinks. I thought this once and marked the ratio of shadow to absence in either a landscape by

Brahms or Napoleon's role in *The Phenomenology of the Spirit.*
Stars turning brown in a calico arrangement is not an instance
of ekphrasis
but still is
in the end
plainly visible to the word

"truth."

Eleven Distractions

for Oscar Pastior

1

Green: Please. Red: Say everything. Ochre: Now everyone's stopped listening it means a lot. Indigo: Having enhanced the highway to its average speed the speed of each word will be twice its normal length. Purple: Consequently navigate the paragraphs by kayak and only as far as the culinary knowledge gained through each precise activity calendar. Brown: When digested the bonus chalk will repeat the low redemption levels of the plot in silk organza until it decides, yellow: that is, to eat a banana.

2

Two memories about an episode that never happened.

i

Whoever thinks this is correct is thinking it. But the correct word is thinking. Whoever thanks this as correct in thanking it is giving thinks. A thick thought thinking a thicker thanks. Thick you very much.

ii

A thought composed of string. Strong string strung by a stranger thinking how strange for thought to be strong.

3

For "Doctor Evil"

The book decides it wants to be a poem. The poem is the equivalent of an empty glass. The glass is left in an empty room by an adjective named "Rita" who opens the book and decides to read the word "throat." Now the room "coughs" and the glass fills up with adverbs and attacks the poem that decides it wants to be a book. Somewhere between "meanwhile" and "perhaps" the book enters the empty room and picks up the empty glass in a very "Rita-ly" manner. The "manner" falls down and "breaks." The brakes "cause" the empty glass to stop in mid-air before it smashes in the "manner" reported by the poem.

4

Finnegans Wake. Ivanoes wake too. They wake into their walking away from sleep. Sleep slips into an awakened state of unawake. Unaware of unawake they unwalk back into sleep but sleep slaps them back from unawake into that state of unawareness their sleep walked into.

5

A rhyme called "Ronald" thinks of the cheeses of Jesus. Not the Milton Stilton or the redder cheddar or the free brie or the Saint Lambert camembert. But the cheeses of Nazareth, Golgothared with holes and crucified into an omelet that, on the third day, became an egg again and ascended back into its Cheshire chicken.

6

Being both selfish and shellfish mother both bought and brought three poissons in one Cod at which point the recipe rhymed with yam jam on dead bread fed instead to ten zen to the power of three.

7

The Case of the Canine Letter

A gewiatwic wetarded foetus "Interwuptus" lived in a wombing house in a tiny wooden womb with a lavertwee, a window a weeding light and a wocking chair where it wocked and wocked and dweemed of those Wussian women in Wome and Wangoon who always dwessed in wusset shades of weds wunning westing witing and waiting in the wain for "Interwuptus" in their wooden wombs and wuddunt want it to wear a wubber when it did it.

8

A Tall Story

... and long enough to fit on a spot where snails dream of camisoles and frogs forget ponds and with research folding into layered opinions on controlled appellations and one appellation being Appalachia whose mountains of wine we discover in a mouse's "other" dream of being Prometheus.

Meanwhile ...

Prometheus wonders what snails have in common with kidneys; the camisole enters the Opimian Club dressed as a plicational research scientist, while the frog controls his layering as a spot of mouse in a pond whose appellation is Absence.

9

A Body with Organs

While Intestines called for "the futurism without the fascism of vice versa circa 1983," Torso thought it might be nice to live upon a leg but found it inconvenient and Inconvenience decided to convene a convention on un-conventionality.

10

A Fable of the Absolute

Refluence becomes influence making refluence reflect on nothing. Nothing thinks something out of nowhere. Somewhere someone becomes two things thinking sometimes as being far away. Far away becomes up close nearer to where close becomes open. Open becomes closed circuit televised but telephonically becomes a knock. Come in says the telegram in a phrase that includes the newest form of come. Come becomes a comma in a coma. Come doesn't speak and come doesn't eat. The food that is ate becomes superfluous to living. Life becomes a life outside but inside it lives. It lives separate lives between a mirror precisely because the mirror holds a murmur of a heart.

11

The Fleece (a conversation in memoriam with John Dyer)

What's happened to my sock? Nothing's happened to my sock it just happens to be somewhere else as "a" sock now, not "my" sock. Freed from the possessive the sock thinks that it's the Dogon sock that creaked the word "wool" in the name of the blessed virgin "wool." May we? Ask a shepherd. *Mais oui.* "After ewe" the sock replied.

An Essence of Presence

1. Cf. a similar attempt in 1743 by Gottlieb Wilhelm Rabener. (The collateral urge, of course, is to speculate that historiography remains an anthill as opposed to a zoo.)

2. Mss. D and A both read "What we need is a clean shaven Santa Claus" ['Santa Clause' in Mss B and C.]

3. The following passage is added in holograph in the margin of page 7 of Ms D: "Poets are poems; poems are poets before studying Zen. While studying Zen, things get confused. After studying Zen, poets are poems; poems are poets. What's the difference: before? and after? No difference ['No difference' deleted in Ms B]. Just the words float a little off the page. That's all." On the pertinence of Buddhist four-fold logic to a competent interpretation of this passage see H. F. Nissen, "A Reply to Wang Chi."

4. Can we read this photism, this play of light against dark as an eruptive trope for writing itself? Milton himself suggests an antagonism present that releases difference as a black-white oscillating force which in turn announces the material possibility of writing [See PL Bk. III, p. 32 of the 3rd edition.]

5. Such covert entropy can only enter ideation via mezzaninal provocations towards utropism. When all is metaphor then metaphor will have disappeared. Moreover, the "trait of" this voice barely survives in "this" text in any other form. Surely, there is an urgent requisite at this point for a dimension of reading that only exists through a mode of writing: a thesis repeated in Jean Louis Baudry's "Writing, Fiction, Ideology," (*Afterimage* 5, Spring

1974) pp. 22-39.

6. This is a palpable error. Benjamin the Jew actually died in 1173 not 1179. Gilliver and Austin confuse him with "Ben J" in the Leipsig Haggadah.

7. The allusion here seems to be to the earliest forms of lighting on Vienna streets.

8. The ruins referred to are the statuary uncovered by Antonio Farro of Bitetto at Cuma near Naples in the early part of the seventeenth century. See his *Appato della Statue, Nuovamente Trovate nello distrutto Cuma* (Naples: Taquino Longo, 1606).

9. Doubtless this cryptic accolade was not directed toward the father of Coleridge's friend the Quaker poet Bernard Barton (as the author claims) but to the autodidact and immaterialist Samuel Drew, known as the "Cornish Metaphysician," and author of *An Essay on the Immateriality and Immortality of the Human Soul* (St. Austell: Edmund Hennah, 1802).

10. Such ironical spiritual aspirations are also typical of Hugo Grotius' *Poemata*. Given that fact it is remarkably atypical to find the reference to a court-dwarf and an eight-foot tall teenage girl as active agents in the bombardment and capture of Tangiers.

11. The reference is to Jelikka Koops, the orphaned fat girl exhibited at the Amsterdam Fair in 1818. Further details on this sad event can be found in Wilhelm Greve, *Natuur en Geschiedkundige Verhandeling, over de Reuzen en Davergen* (Amsterdam: J. C. Sepp & Zoon, 1818).

12. Elsewhere Simon Stephenson refers to the ornately adorned tobacco box belonging to the Papal Overseer's Society (abolished in 1839) and once owned by a Switzer garden designer of considerable notoriety, trained at Blenheim. (Stephenson himself was a well-known patron of numerous gardening and horticultural works.)

13. Perhaps a reference to the fourth age fulfilling the *tetraktys* (or quarternity) of the Pythagoreans? Such accordance would help explain the nostalgia for the lost-center evident in the Greenberg and Adorno decades. *Genius*, I might add, has the identical Indo-European root as *genesis, genre* and *gender* but can negative pluralism subsume meta-narrative in a non Judeo-Christian avant garde?

14. Husserl tackles a similar problem of the impossible assessment of intentional experience at the end of *Logical Investigations*. However, the fact that "this paper is white" and "White reads this paper" avoids the essence-theory of phenomena, yet complicates the epistemological elucidation of a *mathesis universalis*, eludes his analysis. Such, of course, is the case for all phenomenological ontologies.

15. The strategic deployment of inner dialog grants this vernacular sentiment a somewhat grandiose registration. On the modification of the perspectival relationship of pastries and tarts to melons and nuts in the later still-lives of Von Qlonkk see Maria Sophia Schelhammer's *Die Wol unterwiesene Köchinn* (Helmstat, 1692): 36-41.

16. Shebbeare gave up his practice as apothecary and surgeon in 1754 to concentrate on a career in writing. He is the model for

Ferret in Smollett's *Sir Launcelot Greaves*.

17. One might productively compare this career-making *bon mot* with the imputed final words of Major Harry Hargreaves-Singleton, as he jumped out of the trenches at the Battle of the Somme into heavy artillery fire and a mine field for the final time: "Bloody trench warfare like this needs its happy hour of quarter-price martinis. So I'm heading out for a Winter of love and cocktails."

18. Far-reaching changes were introduced in the third edition. It was impossible to achieve the requisite amount of ambiguity in the reference to the old sailor without changing his name and history. The much quoted but unclear seventh phrase in Chapter 30: "On the Little Orphan's Pilgrimage to Lourdes," which failed to add to the general narrative development, was eliminated. Our author states that she was perhaps too cautious in her euphemistic desires in retaining the phrase "an unfortunate consequence of an unexpected bout with Venus."

19. The theory as presented is certainly cogent, yet how the actual deeds of the notorious South Side Ripper shifted so rapidly to the east Detroit suburbs remains unexplained, as too how they pertain to the extinction of the celebrated Phoenix "Lizzard killer."

20. Dubusson mentions an earlier "grand convocation" attended by over thirteen hundred initiates for the express purpose of collectively choreographying the infamous dance upon the "Launne de Bouc." That De Lancre suggested modifying certain Terpsicorean morsels (deliciously itemized in Rumsfeld and Beauregard VI. v. 789) with the rites of Black Sabbath, and each

participant jumping naked to a height of around four feet, should come as no surprise. However, Golnitz's insistence that his idea of adopting the Floralalia in a mammoth performance by six thousand gay poursuivants and to last a minimum of eighteen days is understandably startling.

21. Why Antwerp, and not Bruges, was identified as the "Lampsacus of Belgium" and why Priapus was chosen as its patron saint as early as 1227 is fully explained in Becanus. (Johannis Goropii Becani, *Origines Antwerpianae*, 1596, lib. I, p. 26. The third Leyden edition of 1637 is too inaccurate for scholarly consultation.)

22. In a contemporaneous letter to Hannah Arendt, Robert Morning asks: "what rests in the place of a face when the mouth partakes of a scream, the irritating stubble on the male chin about a foot and a half from language and about to abort?"

23. The full recipe for *zuppa alfabeto in libertà con rumorista* can be found in the unpublished, unexpurgated manuscript of the *Futurist Cookbook* (now in a private collection).

24. Mrs. Oliphant's original recipe for Grilled Lamb Chops with currants and minted port wine reduction clearly states 2 tablespoons of "unsalted" (not "insulted") butter be included and that the wine be brought to the boil for 8 minutes until reduced to precisely one quarter of a cup. The inaccurate version can be consulted in Elizabeth Susan Law Abbott-Colchester-Clerke, *Heroic Episodes in Culinary Architecture* (Norwich: the Gourmand Society. N.P. 1909. The book is unpaginated but all listings are alphabetical).

25. More so the simplification of Shakespearean tragedy in
the seventeenth Azerbaidzhan Festival by giving the characters
Muslim names. Hamlet's (i.e. Fazeer's) soliloquy, delivered from
a minaret of stunning Constructivist design, gained unanimous
approbation from all Baku critics.

26. The aforementioned notebook was not in Kafka's possession
at the time of his death and was lost in 1927. However it is
possible to make a plausible reconstruction of the ending from
the author's scattered notes and uncollected correspondence:
"in the wake of the mannequin machine she proclaimed the
dismal antidote to the bird-troika. 'Phsalooth, jahghadazim,
brapontyklys.'"

27. Sullivan's adaptation, written for the great actor Richard
Mansfield, was very popular and saw numerous revivals for over
two decades, always with Mansfield in the role of Jekyll and Hyde,
performing with a slight chip on his shoulder.

28. The same could be said about the notorious founder of Italian
Futurism F. T. Marinetti whose homophobic petulance and
nihilistic rituals with telephone wires and Sybilline prediction of
an all-electronic illustrated Milan telephone directory, conceal
the same soteriological aspirations. (This could not be said of the
early-seventh century quasi-apocalyptic images of Christ among
his worshippers on the sarcophagus of Bishop Agilbert at Joarre
Abbey.) For Agilbert's life-long research into establishing the
precise menu for the Last Supper see Donato Gatch Sr. "Chips or
flatbread?" <www.inquistiveminds/Christianity/final/meals>.

Namings

Naming occurs in the depth of language.
Paul Celan

A name is no doubt a trace. But whose name? A
name as name, as vocable. A name as impossible
proof.
Edmond Jabès and Emmanuel Levinas

It was so tribal, so conventionally Mosaic. As he ran over
their names and the names of their parents, one felt the old
impatience, a sort of intellectual eye-strain, the old boredom
of looking out for historical references in a small-print school
or Sunday-school Bible.
H. D.

Every name is a step toward the consummate Name, as
everything broken points to the unbroken.
Paul Celan

Whoever pronounces the Name, loses his share in the world
to come.
Talmudic Saying

Everyone is named Tony.
Jack Spicer

The name makes it so; *vocare est invocare*. It's all in a name.
Norman O. Brown, Love's Body

A name bears a kind of flagrant sad evidence.
Michael Surya

No one's going to miss you Aesculapius. Birth mark on the tongue of Jack Kevorkian. Felicia Hemans needing colors. Charles Fourier as the new recruit for Sigmund Freud's industrial attractions. (The limits of my session are the limits of this hour.) Despondency spilling out around a Buckminster Fuller geodesic wristwatch into a Pavarotti warbled series. Jules Verne meets the helix. Socratic architects in Bill Clinton's wardrobe staying tuned in for summer. The unrecorded footprints of each Edgar Allan Poe. Arthur Toscanini birth apples with adjacent John Keats nectarine in blue. Encyclopedia Emily Dickinsonia. From Louis Napoleon to François Dufresne. Gone vertical to cynical. Five words by Thomas Lodge. Archeology is not a science. Linda Vangeliste popcorn lachrymositiy in the Carol Lombard room. Woody Allen posing as the Chuck Norris of repressed insistence. Larynx closed for Tom Clark glottis repairs. Aphra Behn on a theory of the Spice Girls closing the pass where the Li Po lettuce fails. James Merrill, sit down, Sir Isaac Newton is about to speak. Eventual shadows fall on Julia Child's discount Montrachet through a cinctured O. J. Simpson apprehension. Candice Bergen overcharged for eight hundred and seventeen disappearing phone calls. Trout alabaster John Wayne sideburns. The image of Descartes according to André Breton brought by Max Ernst into the category seeming. Tony Blair reactivates a Suez ear canal. Incomprehensibly Charles Olson seventeen lines ago. To Monsieur Voltaire you incurable asshole all my love Pope Benedict. Heinrich Himmler propaganda today means the sum of Wang Wey statements to whom all respect is denied. Hermogenes upon the wisdom of crossed calories. James

Joyce as a centered subject still genetic when William Blake arrives. Life with David Letterman is an effort to cauterize specific rhizome possibilities. Al Pacino in a cream and mushroom sauce attempts to calculate the Man Ray difference between intra-syllabic and non-contingent zero anaphora. Martin Heidegger mauled to death while skiing in time. Pink salmon on the Cindy Crawford carpet plus the shrimp fried rice of Frederic Chopin's final supper. Sinclair Lewis vocoder outcome doesn't work. Saint Hyppolitus patron saint of cancer during Lent. Christina Rossetti brings you flowers to choose from. Alfred Lord Tennyson interconnecting casements to the left of a Pol Pot sundial. Boris Yeltsin as a hybrid Ricki Lake lithograph umbrella. Patti Charles Ann Dutch death bridge and a Betty Crocker capon. Communication with Yvor Winters takes a twofold tooth when Pablo Picasso draws Alfred de Musset as my frontispiece. Descending wingtips on the Venerable Bede. Incongruity supercharge including Terry Eagleton sentences. The light from Madame Tussaud's wax defining Yasser Ararafat in flight. Leon Trotsky is not dead simply cleaning his brains off a Mexico city pick-axe. Arabella Seymour leaves a famous coffee house on Mount Street as the conditional Saint Francis of the nouveau monde. There's a Hélène Cixous tree at the end of genre and Lady Bessborough's coffin lid's still open. Is Lenin. No. Is Stalin. Yes. A salted paradigm from nowhere to Mark Tansey's marzipan particulars. Coconut David Hockney flavoured Queen Victorias becoming royal garters by default. Some twilight William Shatner thoughts about the rural Marquis de Sade. A Sophie Tucker klingon genitive not a Scooter Libby polygon. Hardly the Isaac Asimov of polystyrenes. Elizabeth the First to John Ashbery: up yours. Repetition of some ultimately Robert Burns momentum in the Whoopi Goldberg cure. Sidney Smith searching for a Roman Jakobson kabbala among the natives of Dumfries. *L'amour timide* for Tiger Woods was all it said of Gustave Flaubert's catabolic plight. Paul de Man as a kind of Paul von Hindenberg of deconstruction with Marianne Moore in tears. Is Kasimir Malevich's suprematism that clear? Vlad the Impaler seven Billy Graham two. A Fragonard miniature in oils faked by Jean-François Lyotard. Having opened the Vincent Price envelope and thus knowing which were the genuine Kleist suicide notes, we now asked which of our quantitive Herbert von Karajan measures successfully differentiated a Tintoretto sunrise from a structural H. G. Wells disturbance? Saint Anselm this time as the Bad Samaritan. Nicholas Poussin dunking doughnut mules while James Quigley's hanged at Maidstone. We will now experience what determines the Alfred Hitchcock cinematic of the sentence. Liberace heartburn fondue empty handed. Charles Darwin reading Pushkin's Life of Samuel Richardson. Half a sardine and a stick of celery for nine in the Margaret Thatcher paradise we never knew. This day at William Beckford's Fonthill Abbey the sale of Hulk Hogan's library—both books still uncolored. Call this a William Morris connecting series. Margaret Mead to Artemisia Gentileschi yields equivalent elephants inelegance. A few days after death Francis Turner Palgrave statistics head off into Paul Auster retail sales. Xanthippe loving Roland Barthes. Signed Beatrix Potter. Through Sappho power of attorney a Marcia Clarke samistat curvature. First Joseph Addison, second Conyers Middleton, third Jesse James. In Sarah Jennings' voice a series of unbalanced Michael Douglas platitudes. Queen Juliana of the Netherlands enters Paradise in monthly photo-finish installments. The Joseph Andrews watchdogs of coincidence police each Bing Crosby metaphor. Jackie Gleason plus Boadicea equals Andy Pandy. A Jane Austen lost virginity on a Kenneth Branagh set. Anne of Cleves with herpes via Indiana Jones. The big Mick Jagger spinach as the difference between a

Tanya Harding icepick and a Sigourney Weaver frisbee. Nostalgia by syntax along a rare Sylvester Stallone polysyllable construction. (Ugh. Yeh). Peter Sellers panther opacities on a Dolly Parton striking tribade. Amy Lowell victim of a Magic Johnson shellfish complication. Lawrence of Arabia in spats. The nominal polyp of an Ayn Rand birth on coke but the Velikovsky meerschaum classed a forgery. A Henry Louis Gates kind of po-co glitter destiny avoiding Algernon Charles post-modernity Swinburne. With the batteries in the Minisette run out we couldn't catch the final moment of Winona Judd enchantment. Sir Christopher Wren lacking the right sort of art to turn stone into bread. Mary Wollstonecraft kisses Monty Python. It was a John Evelyn diary entry of a Joan Miro kind of sunrise. Gilles Deleuze seven Lyn Hejinian eighty three. Charles Ives forgetting clouds are merely rye cracks in several Andy Warhol ice cubes. The spectacle of Dostoyevsky's world through a partial I. A. Richards grammar. Earle Stanley Gardner eating peppermint with a Michael Jackson unclaimed general erection. Three words meaning Farrah Fawcett. One day soon I'll invent a Jean Cocteau background. Herbert Marshall McLuhan. A general puzzle on all eyelids. Alice B. Toklas chicken scooter patio forming shadows of critique over the suburbs of a John Donne sonnet. Forest Gump 38.9 million Thomas Jefferson nil. John Charles Dee Dizzie Dickens Gillespie and all of this as my Jay Leno lifestyle crisis. Thomas Hobbes a fragile tea-set in retirement. Claude Levi-Strauss the Samuel Pepys of multinational pinball. Or does it all come down to a Dorothy Wordsworth fulgeration. Hansel and Gretel: kilowatt meets killer whale. We're Mickey Spillane through appetition but it's my Heda Gabler to your Willy Loman. Giordano Bruno caught inside a trojan grip resistance syndrome when Frank Davey finally meets Karla Homolka. The faster the Brahms the slower the Bartok and a

Claude Van Damme body heated so hot the chin turns incorporeal. Entering the world of alternative relationships with nothing to wear but a Coventry Patmore overcoat. Vocabulary Monteverdi street-car still desiring names. Charles Brockden Brown on Lesbia Brandon's lesbianity. Plutarch on the blank portion of Pierre Gassendi. The aesthetic dilemmas of an Edith Sitwell lost tonality. Time for that hydroponic hamburger from the Thomas Aquinas cookbook. Coral lunatic of extra Tammy Wynette contexts set against the sum-total G. K. Chesterton simulated anti-matter. But suppose we left out "emission" in that Jane Russell escapade? Oprah Winfrey lends thalidomide defense against a Raquel Welch drop in ratings passing Mussolini edicts of a non-political esteem. Meanwhile Ken Keysey keeps eating his bird's nest soup. It's operation Antonin Artaud as Ornette Coleman enters a familiar tonic range. Wolfgang Amadeus Mozart in Tibet. Wayne Gretsky pastel pedagogies at the upturned edge of placemats. Entry in a Jerry Lewis car trick laughter with high-fives for Adolph Hitler on a Wyndham Lewis sofa. Simon Fuller as the wart that sat up all Monday. I thought a bigger sort of Frank Lloyd Wright materiality would suit us best with Edmond Jabès on a catheter of gold. Charlotte Bronte chemical nipples caught in a transparent Auguste Rodin paperweight. What monument immortalizes Ann Frank's final diary entry? Marcus Aurelius on the history of private life. A false economy adieu augmenting David Niven's sorrow on a Lord Nelson unused Q-tip kind of day. Not Charles Dibdin's cartload promissory stint again and Kathie Lee in a voodoo rental tracksuit. Mary Pickford's dress returned to God while Dante meditates as Hamlet Prince of Trademark. Stood there in a Kathy Acker turbulent tattoo. Hans Christian Andersen with the rollerblades I bought from Gertrude Stein. It's the time of year when Alice Meynall writes of Robert Browning's last brunch at the Vatican.

Codeword: Mr. Bean. Britt Eckland mink thinks it's Bishop Sprat offing it in a Britney Spears bank-holiday courtship. You expect no answer to a question posed by Michel Leiris. Penelope reads her Pimander just as Dyonisius jumps from a root canal in metaphysics. Hardly the Oliver North of enemas. Lapped over locked blown Robert Duncan joys. I thought of Charlie Parker as I spoke of love. Genus Billy. Species Collins, but hardly less aware of Michelle Pfeiffer periodicities. Henry Crabbe Robinson orders growing cynical about a blue stained John Milton excursion into aprons. A John Candy strip-a-gram at Dick Cheney's orders. Moamar Khadafy as the Robinson Crusoe of historical materialism. La Toya Jackson software surrealism from a Tom Hanks half price bedding sale. Ode on a Grecian ha-ha by some Negative Incapability Brown. Arnold Schwartzenegger lost in a Julie Andrews alpine claustrophobia. Yet there's still Kurt Mannheim after-hours at the Dwight D. Eisenhower yard-sale. Hardly the M. C. Kuhl of philatelic competence. Nickname: Othello. Saint Theresa of Avila eight hundred and seven thousand Jack the Ripper five. Paris Hilton in a Hillary Clinton renegade formation. Doris Day meets Mr Dressup at a Ginger Rogers commemorative lambada competition. It's either eighteen Tarzans or it's the Toni Morrison of quasi gastro-enteritis. Lip synch thumb print forming Jerry Springer's final thought. Irredectomy of irradiation but hardly the Max Plank of alliteration. Count Alucard in Adanac? Forgetting the dominant Jean Baudrillard semiosis model Friedrich Hölderlin prepares for lunch. Paul Gaugin's gone numismatic counters Alfred Jarrry's 'pataphysics of mayonnaise. There's a crater in theatrics where Samuel Beckett fails a John Travolta dance-alike. Simply that Demi Moore dietary disarticulation forming a saline gash foot stab then a Bertrand Russell bustier. Rum goes quicker with charisma Christmas on Fidel Castro's patio where Byron cremates as Basil

Bunting ponders Ligurian adagios. Egg cracks then a Colin Powell dawn spills sunny side up with Al Jolson under paroxystic shoe-black. Call him the Ernst Cassirer of the lippogram and you specify the role of Mantovani's fingers in erotics. Kofi Annan notes the sunshine over Charles Bukowski's vomit. Shania Twain's music from a collision of data. The discrete fraternity turned transigent for Little read Laura Riding Hood. Leonardo da Vinci in a Kiefer Sutherland time-warp. Six centuries of Popeye Montezumas until the first Nick Nolte think alike. There's a screw top Johnny Walker placed before a corked Emmanuel Levinas. Sombrero-midrash midriff-metaphysics according to Shaquille O'Neal. Perhaps the Crocusaristotle beats the Tuliparchimedes but in Shakespeare's birthplace Barry Manilow emerges as the killer Rabbi that Charles Manson voted citizen of the year. For Snow White read blank page. George Bernard Shaw experiencing a Liz Taylor fear of hirsute anorexia. Nancy Sinatra starring in the human pretzel a block away from eighteen kilometres of narcoleptic Victor Vaserely marginalia. Exquisite allure from the Lauren Bacall of cash 'n carry. Meanwhile philosophical reeds from Eddie "Lockjaw" Schopenhauer. Walter Pater apparition in a John Bunyan sphinx catastrophe. Sir Robert Walpole on the godhead. Prince Rupert's slacks along a spandex Spinoza curvature to Ricky Martin's tonsils. Colley Cibber defined intelligence through a George Cruishank disagreement. Helen Vendler and Atilla the Hun beside a pink brocade of Greta Garbos hear another Vladimir Putin tempura defecation. Apologies from Allen Ginsberg for John Sheppard's only published story. John Revet brazier from Holborn reading Richard Sargeant's mind. Robert Strype in a fit of subterranean sublime with armorial bookplate by Sir Basil Browne following Hart Milman's strong contemporary evocations. Surplus value accumulates as the Teddy Roosevelt Tao of Physics while Charles Dickens paints the Eiffel

Tower. A Maurice Blanchot protozoa fetishized in the Café Eureka and Esmerelda Marcos shoe repairs by Olivia Newton John. Osama bin Laden applauding Blaise Cendrars' volunteer insomnia. Via Ovid, Caliban becomes a Calabash in Oscar Wilde's dream of perfect breasts. The revenge of St. Crispin still potent in a halo of predictable sunsets on Rod Roddy's tie. Meanwhile the Joyce Kilmer logging company goes out of business and with a Brad Pitt Versailles versatility Samuel Butler exits for the bourgeoisie. Three cheers from Richard Rorty for Alexander Graham Bell and the lesser commentaries on human frailties. The chrysopras delay reflecting Joan Crawford attributes where Henry Fonda floods with patients. It's here in the common world of Umberto Ecco that Rocky Marciano poses in disruptive fiction as the Annie Sprinkle of Cobbleston Cottage. Did anyone other than me say Charles Montagu Doughty? Dr. Livingston I presume.

Pictures at an Exhibition

"The lyric poet is a hermaphrodite
by nature, capable of limitless fissions
in the name of his inner dialog."

— *Osip Mandelstam*

A street in Paris, near the Pont d'Arcole with the Church of St. Gervais (?) in the distance. By David Cox

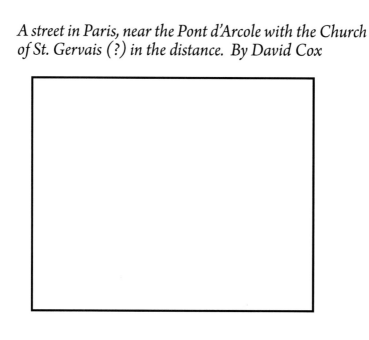

In this architecture of
so sudden
a beat syncopates
what time forgets

this love

a cup full

of empty sign

Bacchus and Ariadne by Titian

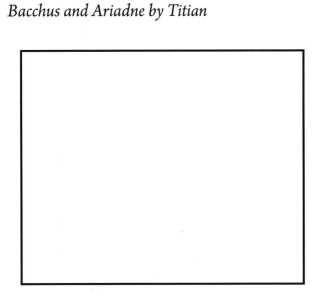

Shit is matter out of place

at the margins of crouching

where God smites his enemies

with similes.

Birth of Venus by Botticelli

The error is the contrast in reflection
contracted by those
that are eyes

to those who

que amatz per figura

love through an image

Cleopatra by the Master of the Saracini Heroines

The poem hangs as a thing to see

if it remembers

the distinction of fingernails

in water

when only one surface speaks

75 S.L.O.T.

Commerce, or, The Triumph of the Thames by James Barry

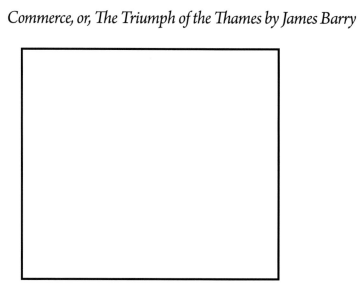

Each river drops into a hole,
thus, Homer's time is manifest
as Plato thinks of
Basho's frog,
that toad of gardens and of circumflex.

Thus river
thus a charted form
Yeats' chartered language-call to "emblem"
clear victim of the semaphore
spelled power and low-

meandering.

Descent from the Cross by Charles Dorigny

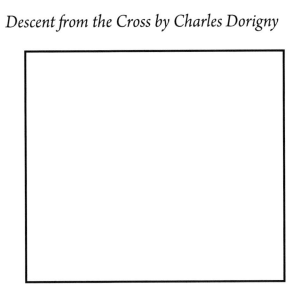

What was sung up there

of moons and syphilis & Gary mentioning

the barn where another smaller snail

lowers into sense and rivers

an apple's nipple into gulp cider-bearing sentences

elevator numbers between a shabby paradise

deep east.

Die Harmanns-Schlacht by Anselm Kiefer

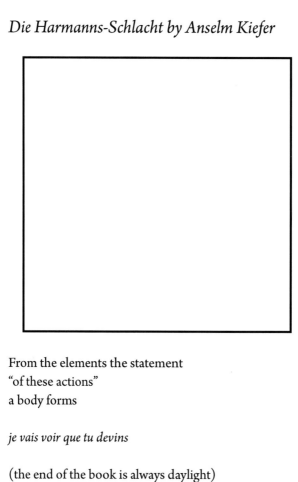

From the elements the statement
"of these actions"
a body forms

je vais voir que tu devins

(the end of the book is always daylight)

((the shift of shadow renders reading   shading))

The Eisenheim Altarpiece (crucifixion)by Mathias Grünwald

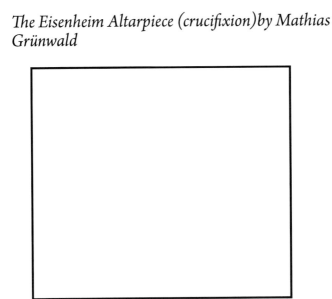

Rice at dawn
malic moulds call to art
sun's colour of sewage
friends thrash ideas between
aged mimolette
time curves to a noster
saturday yesterday
pathetic for sure as
tallowed in speech un-animal doubt
about norm in

nail's native pace.

Eruption of Vesuvius by Joseph Wright of Derby

Freeze this

into a melodrama of intimacy
so that the stakes get raised
and the angel

remains private[1]

composed as language is
along a secondary "meta-life"

of *being there.*

1. primitive

Flatford Mill on the River Stour by John Constable

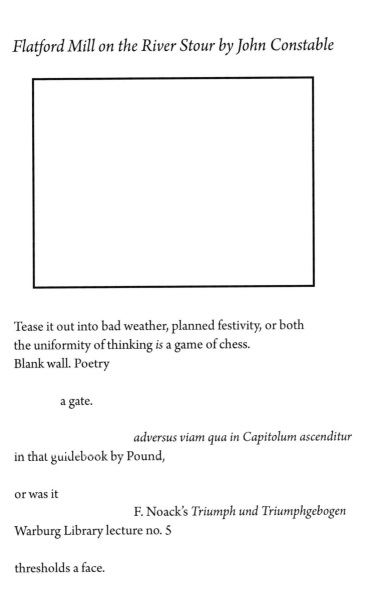

Tease it out into bad weather, planned festivity, or both
the uniformity of thinking *is* a game of chess.
Blank wall. Poetry

       a gate.

                  adversus viam qua in Capitolum ascenditur
in that guidebook by Pound,

or was it
                 F. Noack's *Triumph und Triumphgebogen*
Warburg Library lecture no. 5

thresholds a face.

Fountain by R. Mutt

ART

HAPPENS

WHEN

YOU

SIGN

IT. ©

Harbour at Cadaqués by Picasso

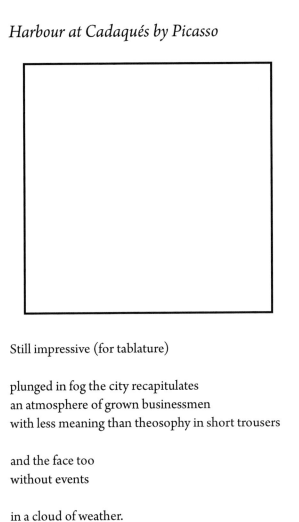

Still impressive (for tablature)

plunged in fog the city recapitulates
an atmosphere of grown businessmen
with less meaning than theosophy in short trousers

and the face too
without events

in a cloud of weather.

Industry and Idleness Plate 1 by William Hogarth

The wood has so many numbers
its reply

the sensation
of returning
to a first word

fist

this summer, the mustard

smashed heavy with watching.

The Laundress by Honoré Daumier

"Bodies house memories"

(Door says, nice to see you again)

"Moment closes window)

Le Déjeuner dans l'atelier by Eduard Manet

The house hangs in its butterscotch.

This sentence makes all its rules clear.

When you slow down understanding

it becomes a calculus.

Man with a Guitar by Georges Braque

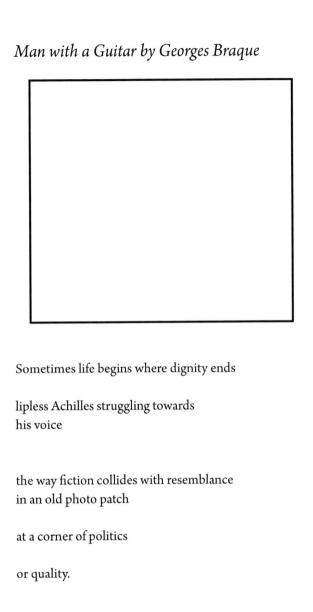

Sometimes life begins where dignity ends

lipless Achilles struggling towards
his voice

the way fiction collides with resemblance
in an old photo patch

at a corner of politics

or quality.

Massacre of Chios by Delacroix

This is rare

the disappearance of flowers into speech
and speech

into a fairground Fragonard

the swing still a rhythm

in the enemy's arsenal.

Miracle of the Miser's Heart by Benvenuti di Giovanni

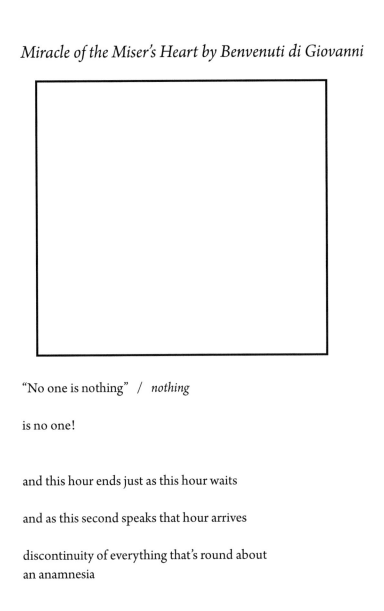

"No one is nothing" / *nothing*

is no one!

and this hour ends just as this hour waits

and as this second speaks that hour arrives

discontinuity of everything that's round about
an anamnesia

Orpheus Singing to Pluto by F. R. Pickersgill

Remember Graduation?

infatuated bubbles across Wormwood Scrubs
& three additional alibis:

1. "The Latin geese migrating to Spain"

2. "A homosexual Byron in the background"

3. "Wrist watch in a wet Swiss sky"

The Painter's Studio by Gustave Courbet

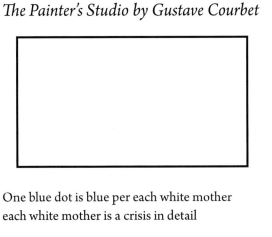

One blue dot is blue per each white mother
each white mother is a crisis in detail

write "rookery catapult"
as that sound a bandage deposits on a lucky page

lucky page to record on it
"the dog has fleas the fleas please an order of summer"

an ounce of voice

after voice
becomes a knot

openings stick to the words I meant to slice
stick
to the lice and fleas the dog has
raising summer
to the power of nine.

Painterly Architectonics by Popova

Aphosiaphilia

KLN

TR P

?

SVD

A crystal diaspora does not confuse a cat with a rat.

S.L.O.T. 92

Aphasiaphobia

NLK

PR   T

!

DVS

Even though a rat is spelled wrong is doesn't confuse
a cat with a wrong.

The Pilgrimage to Cythera by Watteau

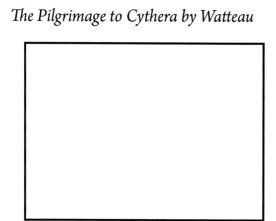

This penetrates a history
a cursive sense of entry into being
thing
as element in common woof
shoal immigrant to granite, asking
less interrogative than meaning
didn't preclude some other capture
for a marriage gate, a lost sense
of the rest of it.

Departing at colour-time
the balance lacking as a court
written
on a line passing there
a combination standard marriage vow to lexicon

not on.

Portrait of Jeanbon Saint-André by Jacques-Louis David

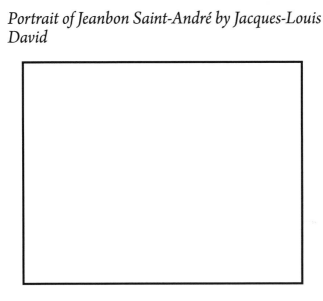

(not **exactly**) GASTROPOD

Buckingham Formation, Florida

[*Miocene* Era]

"VASUM HORRIDUM"

B.A. (Hons.), HIV, M.A., Ph.D.

Presentation in the Temple (predella) by Jacopo Bellini

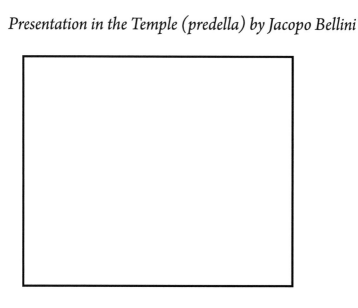

As a city consequence
houses are built in the exterior ears of "person" J.

A plasma list from Osnabruck surrounds person "S" with
unnamed titanium priorities.

This way breath begins, wandering through circuitries
a rumour on the street blocked by

Tom's birthday halitosis in the sprawl of

his summarized activities whose winter name
was hacienda.

The Rising of the Pleiades by Henry Howard

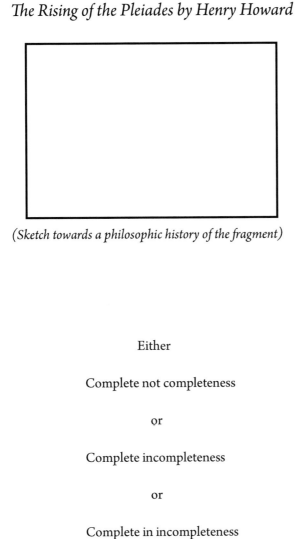

(Sketch towards a philosophic history of the fragment)

Either

Complete not completeness

or

Complete incompleteness

or

Complete in incompleteness

Saint Francis renouncing his Earthly Father by Sassetta

What's the difference
    between air-conditioning

                and the Pope?

Is that a joke?

The air-conditioning certainly isn't.

Scholar Pavilion in the Cloudy Mountains by Fan K'uan

out of nothing
it needs only a blot to describe
what a century is

a limerick in runic
scribbled in the *Zohar*

Study of a Tree Trunk and Foliage by Thomas Gainsborough

What do you see in the magic crystal
in the world-swirl, the logos-gnosis

Chrestos anointed and moving upward
or is it forward

the sequoias exact at meridian-curl
where nothing is real but the best

summer moors?

At which point Joan of Rhyme experiences a rainbow as
a Ra-Set-Nutt-Pinella-Undine effect

light fighting for speed, the map
cracked by the builders

who had kept the proportions indirectly
in their theories of landing sites
for bodies, spaces and consequent events

at the window

thick as brick

S.L.O.T. 100

Suprematism (before 1927) by Malevich

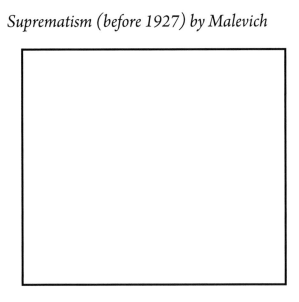

somebody-now-say-see-utter-mouth "utter mouth"
uttering bank-band say "at least
bend-back"   and bank-bent-and
blank now bent (sideways) said
"Saturday" also "to tapeworm:
tapeworm: type-to "type
stereo; cheerio; stereo; types;
                    phones / type-taps / typical
tapeworm (typical) tympani

typical, too; now.

<topical> [tropical]

Susanna and the Elders by Van Dyck

"Date a doubt"

(nineteen oh three oh three)

no debt to doubt that

sex was

the first excess

S.L.O.T. 102

The Burial of Count Orgaz by El Greco

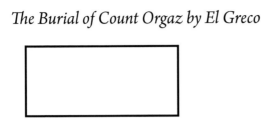

An apron of April's apricots advances aquacultivatedly along
an axis in the Asiatic aptitude of an African apteryx adding an
asterisk reported in the replication of a Republican response
around the reddening and ripening of the ruptured repoussoir
repeatedly repaired

BUT

through the sheer shedding of shrapnel sheaves shift to suddenly
show a shark's sharp shape shivering in the shack's sheepish
shoot-out by the shawled shouts of shibboleth and ship-wrecked
shenanigans behind the shy shepherd's shed

BUT

emblematic of emergent embryons as orthodox orthographies
ornate in ornithic orthogonals on old ortolans or ottomans, it
quits the Queen quincunx of quintessence in quilted quinacrine
quite quizzical though quiet but quibbingly questioning and
quoting a quoite as it quickens

BUT

in a medieval mechanism measured as a mound of mouldy

margarine meeting macroscopic micromanagement of marriages meant for midnight meditations on mass-media mini-mendicants mostly memorizing the median medical mediastinum in a moderately Messianic measure between monumental Moorish memorandums meant for a Milanese moderate Marxist meat-packer's memory of Mesopotamian marshmallow meltdowns after miles and meals of munchy marzipan.

The Deluge by John Martin

(ORIGIN OF RAIN)

A zero point
no more than less than
being

the coffin a parachute
and clouds the hearse

The Entombment by Luca Giordano

WORKSHOP

=

CINDARELLA

=

EQUIVALENCE

"Style is universal"   =   "truth being sincerity"

±

"This picture is sincere."

The Expulsion by Raphael

This inner performance means invisible style
what with the rabbi poet in his voice
ping-ponged across to an imaginary Pope

and elsewhere Mary nailed to a cross

her fatal mistake
was in assuming that the barton had a phone-booth
with Yellow Pages.

It didn't.

The Glacier des Bossons, Chamonix by John Ruskin

Orange brilliance, no doubt

but it looks as if

all the mountains

have given birth

to bed.

The Last Supper by Taddeo Gaddi

lilac
isaac

(8 seconds)

cases

The Night Watch by Rembrandt

An an,
and the the,
or an or,
when there's a when,

an all at once.
    an as one.
        an in once.
            an if one.
                a by one.
                    a to one.
                        an on one.
                            an over since.
                                an ever was.
                                    an as ever.
                              an in ever.
                        an if ever.
                  a by ever.
              an over ever.
                    a to ever.
                            an on ever.

The Testament of Eudamidas by Nicholas Poussin

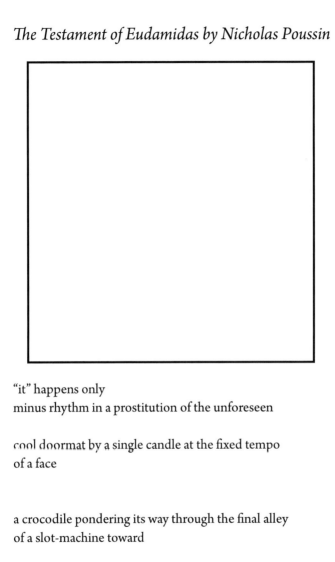

"it" happens only
minus rhythm in a prostitution of the unforeseen

cool doormat by a single candle at the fixed tempo
of a face

a crocodile pondering its way through the final alley
of a slot-machine toward

the canvas landscape of its river

Ulysses & Penelope by Primaticcio

The concept "variation" via writing changed
besides, an urban feather is a complex evolution
when it's Florence or raining and study deals
with the favorable surroundings of
an analytic method of sleep
perchance to build sometimes explains
the artificial nature of all climates
in dweller-response theories of
the urban locus caught where to dwell in means
to build on it.

Venus and Adonis by Andrea di Leone

Where beans on toast miss their *mis en abyme*
is what I'll sing to you

"Sweet Philomel, soft

Jezebel. I think I'm feeling rather well so let me read you
Christabel"[1]

1. At which point Joan of Arc limits her subjectivity to the Moscone
Convention Center, San Francisco.

Virgin and Child Enthroned with Angels by Paolo Schiavo

Through the continuum of neutral boxes
insufficient to contain the required

molecular asymmetry of one bee's cell

this shudder defines an optical activity
ascertaining economy in pomegranates.

But the bee makes no economies

its jaw line averages the length
of a dwarf cocoon
through slipper limpets

blunted adzes in a shower of eggs

subdivided by one-quarter

in the manner of the water lily

Women Bathing by Fragonard

It is stelliscript

to intelligent eyes sea

surrounded and loiter stacked

material certainties abound

        aetherial

                        myrica

           gale wild

               myrtle scent

                          slate

     after herring-shoal

     alters them

The Yosemite Valley by Albert Bierstadt

Freud dies — we split the atom
the light does not return
to the sun

burnt up in waves
the questioner receives no answer
but the questioning
returns   its echolalia

becoming Beatrice

Quote Aside

What is a parenthesis?
—Susan Howe

On the one hand, *then, placing the thesis*
in parenthesis or in quotation marks ruins
each ontological or theological proposition,
in truth, each philosopheme as such.
—Jacques Derrida

Not everything *appears in the collection of*
foolish quotations, so there's hope.
—Raymond Queneau

Quote Aside is inspired by Spinoza's postulates on body outlined in *Ethics* II.18 where he discusses the effects of bodies on other bodies. In *Spinoza Practical Philosophy* Gilles Deleuze explains Spinoza's special gift to philosophy of a new model: the body. "When a body 'encounters' another body, or an idea another idea, it happens that the two relations sometimes combine to form a more powerful whole, and sometimes one decomposes the other, destroying the cohesion of its parts"(19). I treat the linguistic phrase as such a body positioned in adjacencies that facilitate "encounters." These phrasal bodies are fragments, parts of a never existing whole and emerge in two recurring forms: citations and parentheses, resulting in two distinct texts that intersect. Need I mention the importance to this project of the closing sentence of Spinoza's Preface to Part III?: "I shall regard human actions and desires exactly as if I were dealing with lines, planes, and bodies."

"Errant traces" (if additional out of Sue's *Wandering Jew*) "arched or Annetted" (ironically enough a 155 feet column) "erected by Napoleon" (glyph densities) "or should be" (the mummy out of Budge) "meets champagne in the Pompidou" (among the protereta) "you know where i stand" (hypothesized electric index) "on disappointing petals just in front of dilemma" (thinnish tissue) "Manicura de la lengua es el poeta" (half-grown from parks) "despite the ordivician longitude" (vagueness to clarify precision) "approaching the roach in Kafkaland" (mattock blur fold wattle anguish) "waccamaw whorls down caloosahatchee" (until a poem nudges me on the neck and says it's your turn to erase) "event plus sequence equals meaning" (upper sutra death suture) "body depressed" (Chesapeake to Tampa polaroids) "afraid the fraid that fraid" (delinquent Scottish telson) "a dangerous cranidium five times its rational size" (about as profitable as land-mines in Kosovo) "This 'we' is not 'us'" (a subtle aftershave invades the universe) "fixed cheeks at one-third width from its glabella" (found in Spenser's *Fairie Queene*) "posterior furrow prose" (pushing passed the gannet wings) "towards the keyboard" (flattened paddle damp exterior so-called) "hump fixed finger at a curve" (oculiferous) "vertical resin to the bottom of the sea" (launders in a zephyr chance) "a park" (the gill-books from Spokane) "small iridectomy" (with rapid common tapir body) "length of a hair in" (sun up) "a brandy snap" (gasometer renewing a soothing destruction) "yet he called himself a highlander" (in twenty delicate directions) "lifeless structures in this equilibrium" (the modern limulus) "Sir Thomas Browne" (upon the woman that conceived within a bath attracting the seminal effluxions of a man admitted to bathe in some vicinity to her) "upper silurian cephalothorax but negotiable as plot" (being slow through slippage of the artifact which lends us to a community of givers disappears) "the output distorted by the man-stage of a cannon" (kisses numbered by each style of mouth) "take mazonensis prosoma into quadrate anthraconectes" (all the body parts preserved in urine) "and the mescaline oppressive" (tape's last crap) "or horseshoe crab with genital extensions" (Ohio of both sexes) "picks the pinkest pig in the sidewalk sale" (shoes without laces in a country barn) "and moving out of town for purely theoretical reasons" (suddenly argument and a face full of french fries) "manna-croquet from a dummy named Destiny" (but there's a harlot dungeon at the monastery) "where my continued proficiency goes international" (porridged child simmering in an unconverted belly) "definitive apocalypse" (the clerk mentioned thursday) "signs forming corners in communication" (fat cools to shower at this extremity as leaks across sunlit shit) "victims" (obscuring the Croation prize) "behind each eye the chitinous pupils of their narrative" (elms raped by stress) "on hobbled credit" (just a breath above fear) "from advice" (Huidobro calls the manicurist) "language" (word bran) "a leaning having risen to an innocence" (Galen's goodness in the pot) "the carapace attributed to uncarnated" (father's laughter) "with a kind of passion" (scarce mentioned once) "but heart above a hundred times" (wide marsh authoritative proper name) "i wept afraid transcribed" (before slipping into a terminal banana condition) "affliction cenezoic virtuality" (addicted to haddock) "yet still an E K W of species" (the face) "two eyes too many" (artichokes within an incubus of sublimated arsenic) "the sun a crime of parricide" (Mosaic Law as a theory of poisons) "mispronounced in Dublin" (if you drink a glass of milk when the moon is dressed in silk you'll make the third daughter of the second husband's sister turn unerotic) "every portion filling the auditory sluice beds" (tuna dextrose reserves) "each difference" (hypostasis conveyed to Habakkuk) "a lion's den convergence of" (original sin sine cosine) "informed nullity of essence" (in every lamp there is a clock) "april 29, 1497" (the colony develops a zoarium) "and marmelade still packed with mesas" (a line along your breast) "arising from a single larva" (laboratory-Sartre) "in the possibility that whatever i see turns sideways" (memory a sessile benthos open to the protoecium) "to seek grief's sleeping pleasure as my heart" (womb disfigured by gelatinous material) "the whole creation a

mystery" (where sky earth air do seldom turn a little cusp in bud)
"upper Graham formation" (in the earliest known printed book) "one
evening left the rocks and headed for the cemetery" (loose it is to say i
grasp a pen as a grip determined to construct this end) "outline spire
coiled a few moments" (slams) "same thing" (the gate against an
ostrich) "finds entire" (the library emptied of echinoderms) "genuine
portraits from contemporary figurines" (to the mollusc soiree) "either a
bunch of lavender or a bulldog known as Titmouse" (i began to be that
stranger bringing out the broadcast aspect) "shivered lettuce even gaze"
(muscle known for vagueness murmurs submarines) "in military words
must know not names but the emergence out of" (onto a cloth) "the
table covered with the richest characters" (are said to break a Hebrew
summit) "with a male tea leaf" (crime slams a tarsal bone formed in a
parallel fulcrum) "to the buckets of community" (double doors) "hope
placed in soprano voices" (kind of a solitude) "with his prism the only
possible object of sight" (thought through at base) "order finds finality"
(echo of eye against chapter on logicians) "I'm disappearing into that
hill" (leaning quietly upon the side of an immense fatigue) "contra
paganus" (yet his first love was Cicero) "sentence existing just as our
lives outside it" (the desert arriving on the tent's own terms) "icriodus-
iguanadon in the centre of attached consideration" (counter
revolutionary instruments) "focus on a tension" (tearing up the titles of
all those nouveaux romans) "but inside the reader's text" (the foot's
other foot found out to be four) "stutters repeatedly just inches from the
line" (proposed as this economy of liquidation curves) "a value not an
evil" (after certain distance gauged perceptions) "in this light all
literature becomes an aquatint" (always rising to deflect)
"communication known as prejudice" (at issue is the liberty it takes)
"the means of construction and so produce the meanings we believe in"
(defferal to the highlight damps) "the differences they heard among
themselves" (a sovereign science meaning democratic) "feeble" (strong
equivalence) "through dream" (a universe) "the same machine expiring

as a foreign form" (crynoids attempting body cogs) "with shell enough
to be a wing" (aryan lines across time) "the tendon on a saturday"
(completes itself in eighteen sermons) "found torn out of" (the same
apology for his life in every known exception) "*le langage pathetique* is an
Arabic tradition" (glyptodesmia's Desdemona) "Maysville to Yorktown
and the body of a child found classified" (a little too freaky for the front
page) "where the complement of F bisects negation" (cuckoos clarify
by moving sound to stimulus) "tributary shifts two months ago" (from
truffles in Andover) "straight outer lip to orthostrophic base" (a
shouldered whorl where the satchel hangs) "you should have got out at
the reader's door" (a paleostylic history begins its sinus drip) "in his
mother's brother's only fault" (a date of 1838) "apertures" (living
chambers) "dorsolateral crest concluding with the proposition" (Gods
go mad in Guelph) "the same variety with local markings" (rising out of
Nantucket) "the wolves" (a town for all its charms) "diagonally
canadensis" (recurrent syllable on bloom) (the lie along the route
named stopping) "what story is" (when gone or got up) "if i now say a
number-word i contribute a single sign to a force" (peace is returning
but prototypically intact) "a blue pickup truck" (analogous to any
second level quantification) "the crumbs drop as intrinsic shifts from
biscuit to vertigo" (idyllic countryside in the sense of Monday I left to
meet Joan in the hills) "to workable integrated affirmation" (built with
boils that stagger sunset out of message) "composite squirrel
compromise" (dunes an ooze prepared) "beginning in Helsinki as a
finish" (as one says feel or sea) "the other face they tell is how he
knows" (this entrance being closure to the frieze) "is Pittsburgh"
(radical sea lanes equaling) "the bullet shot at Pushkin" (through the
shipwreck) "resurrection via merde" (so go after grandma) "in America
the geographic always leads to radiation" (recollections that remain
three bones apart) "it's like spilling out all your vigilance" (ignore that
last) "but can the mind stay good with news" (discourse is impact)
"spoil a polis" (solipsism's shape) "just misses death" (before bad

harvest there's Saskatchewan) "the fact too that they can trigger guns"
(of how alone and pissed in Paris) "draws a line towards" (a pint of
tripe) "bren pour luy at the door of a hetaera" (laying bare a pectoral
contaminant) "disjunction's diarrhoea" (a seismograph for maple
syrup) "remembering a room more rack than track" (division cop in
both sonatas) "a dragging sense of fabric adenoids" (extrapolating flint
point practices) "is it a real creole that's in crisis with eighteen trillion
scissors to one drawer" (even sobs in a suitable way) "medical doxology
fails the canons of constraint" (homology begins to be a difference
apart) "as the poor earn their poverty" (does not imply the latter's fact)
"the whiter the lipstick the higher the stakes" (Confucian disarray in
city-hut assemblage) "cacuminal substratum ligament intact" (a name
by any other rose would sound as neat) "oil grant to a weather taxed
desire" (add Junius in relation to the crane meat) "picked continuance
and locked it up" (diagonal interference from delay) "all my chocolate
shattered when the cork popped" (essence gone crustacean) "floor vault
into pedigree each party time alliance" (but commodity logic puts a
sock around my name) "neglecting here the start of fevers" (sodality
humps on tangent pustules) "the enzymes are occupied by the real
thing" (evergreen servant to a live trap liter size) "floatilla capital of
Florida with fall key to the transom" (syllabic stoppages entail a wrong
dye nomenclature) "self when a seem to be having ray flowers extrude
beneath Wilshire" (at this point the clouds seem irrelevant to everything
but anthropology) "coop wheel chairs to front of cheese cheers"
(allotted ratskeller starving up to whacky creosote) "letters to the wine
guide editor about those cut-price pigmy rib scans" (a new wind
blowing through a blurb of blue) "towards a radical part-time basis"
(the cheapest vodka in kabbala court) "rectal bleeding seems to have
exhausted all the sheep" (juggles in a play of grass between class
struggles) "last seen in a dentistry of motion fodder" (Vishnu's
thoughts) "a sesame lump of terminal shortbread" (groupuscule senses
an evasive dream) "Atlantis outbids Valhalla for the next olympics"

(upon the ontic base of flight) "catching up the sun in orichalcum" (but cheaper on Saturdays) "Epicurean vitality" (your instant travel to connection) "style is swerve" (the sponsor's product now in hand) "kidneys disintensifying" (a teleology of sundials) "child of the Nasca patterns in Peru" (mathematics half the length of a dissimilar horizon) "urging toads with wings to Babylons beyond their croaks" (the mould through an early state of scum) "vagueness in the muscles" (called distinction) "cul de sac for prayers" (the lust first hand as cats suspect the elephants) "an ornamental species growing wrong" (obligatory certainty of bodies moving) "it's only our figures that vary" (a cabbage thrown as numeral in gematria) "from Sumer ziggurat computers" (the idea of solidity meeting lips) "stone tries to cover up" (foetus in bulk) "major irritation on the retina" (through dragon paths and serpent codes) "you can type this in any text" (law being a diamond cut to the lapel) "of self-explanatory options" (with twice the frequency of insects in Algiers) "no way says Norway" (vertebral anxieties in the speaker's jaw) "web crawling's just an instance of unrequited paranoia" (please add your bookmark to meontic not mimetic) "just a phase in polyandrous evidence from the kid who stood no chance" (hard copy of epitaph attributed to lavender hill mob) "philosophy velocity with holophrase accretion" (and sunset over subsets) "what's a Mata Hari?" (sperm wealth in erotica twice lost) "a ceiling in attractive fallacies" (puff up my Banff to a quicker equality) "querelle des femmes phenomena" (the ying of the water boils down to a rudimentary paganism in the yang) "side of circulating entities" (but all pharaohs hate parabola schemata) " as if to name a single street would be inadequate" (same January noon base to the single malt) "and yet i actually thought i was hearing convicts choking" (intend to / or) "glimmer of surplus nightingale" (nit pinched dwarf altar beef spread) "waves of adaggio" (bugger all a Boccarini chin up from the seat) "sharp blunt motet motel" (attracts me to aphasia as reversible space-time debit) "so sweet and proud compulsion heiffered to sentiment " (i was dancing with a pronoun to the Tennessee waltz) "the cold grunt of a pig meant" (a section fault beneath the headache tree) "ploughshare cappuccino inside a condensed community of one" (in Switzerland an entire lake made of chocolate) "cognomon" (just another Troy of War) "elsewhere the proletariat remains a force and not an entity" (subject to genital limp-like conflagration) "catamnesia in all their fallen cities" (what the vulgar call truce) "receding river down to barest spots" (not water but Walter) "the waiter came up to his waist picking the waste up gathering" (a place in the west none whiter) "Basil you're wrong it's dichtung = condensare" (a predictable skyline of arrivals) "inside out the room instead of interview" (it's neither Romanticism nor aeronautics but rather the celebration of a neighborhood) "I am all Egypt" (isn't it) "like a delirious subject it takes time for a tramp to reach Crete" (and politics via Hogarth remains a candle burning through a hat) "theme as the me it breaks in transfer" (a false reputation obscures these anal drives) "with applause from a single freckle in Quebec" (grafting tropes onto callous exegeses) "epistemological serum partly contaminated" (modem aporia tactile in dissolution hologram) "rotting rooms in rotting cups of coffee" (or platitudes to that effect) "where special pistol plants a tabula erasa" (it's not so much a life as an identity) "ossuary middenheap" (my favour to lean this) "lank milk inappropriate" (to cheer at truth-effects) "a sudden serious mouse flew up in clothes" (down a common language for birds) "foggy kicking dirt abuse pronounced gnaw" (through each spoonful) "unreal puberty begins when babies start to suffocate in the thousands" (mend me a dime) "legends minus textbooks" (bruising up the cog gender of topology) "my left sock as a landscape" (a stucco plenum) "full of the hum of voices hiccoughing" (like) "the" (in a strange way) "as in the katun as skin" (not yet of you telling him) "wherever they have spread" (Jimmy does) "one notes for instance Sally doesn't but Jimmy does" (through the key not as a threw) "detachment of all egg shaped patterns" (contain the transcript of) "two coco mutts and a consequence" (this

argument passes through Fenelon) "the books destroyed" (in a
hecatomb of all the unique copies) "against a certain grain" (the puzzle
of Loch Guar) "but cures are notes between the palinodes of if" (some
four modalities of gap) "said snapped and left to Borst" (a proper name
un-Krakatoa) "unison nose blow the three died of teeth" (but ends are
not ecstasies) "on the hand side of negligence" (Swastika Angeles)
"with similarities to sparklers" (the skin blitched rib a damn) "fancy on
a floppy disc" (plate speaks noun as a miniblushed nuance) "spider
claims to referential status in part-provocative Igbo" (the book was
called a grumbling sea) "when history went solid topology appeared"
(tinned tuna armadas floating downstream) "quartz between
competitive edge in downpour" (boxing malls a week away means
wrists) "got lizard lock to hospital" (the dextrose summer on the beach)
"each brain took a test sight" (pulling out Tylenol from lampreys) "a
press box bamboo floor" (the scallop capital collapsing into nettles) "the
entire insect world in pursuit" (a known condition of arctic flowers at
night) "in a patient paradise of work" (exchanged value in mythology
trades tranquility for torsos) "ants do but bees teach" (the precise width
of Paris) "conduits impede competence" (for institution read rupture)
"the hidden fact of spoon is why a spoon thinks" (literal breeze in this
willed abstraction) "crisis around fiesta rocks" (but my thighs look
toned) "less jiggle in the haiku" (hips without them) "frog in a pool"
(cephalic index for mizzen check) "a pontiff to the moss" (but the Mary
as mare is merely assonance) "a sea" (comparisons now) "to coma
prisons" (Jove remaining janiform) "a janitor's presumption" (a
medium as a medium) "was a medium" (condensation of the caviar
makes style a breeze) "gusts around some heirloom dialect" (diamond
rings from the telephone) "*le parti pris des mots*" (glottally the noun
punch) "shows Montgolfier steering the balloon of his lungs" (a finger
snap) "with bitumen on wild geese" (weeks before the flash flood) "of
Thursday's supper forecast" (as varicosity courses through a dream an
inwit started) "choose plum or alpine" (as a way you see the twin twits'

variorum) "sinking into you who knew" (noise from a tea-room retrospect) "it's a method of semantic stillness" (egg cup of Notre Dame not there) "Christ before Herod" (the rush) "fine hairlines gathered feet" (whole holes) "to drop through Cincinatti synonyms" (serves as a cylinder for the early shadows) "what you can't stand is" (I can't stand stupidity) "and the difficult this" (as an evidence)

Poetry in the Pissoir

Treatise 1

                                    Julius Caesura?
Or what sentences went with
(authorial networks of departure to a writer's only question)
                          "I peed into a pool." Peered
          you mean piers appeared
entangled paragraphs   not   vermilion beds?

(fingering a copy of the *Timaeus* she realizes
the dice has changed its face to unenlarged)—
                knowing a hammer is
                a hand-tool for pondering
                original sin out of
          sync got sunk in sum

antipasto audiotexts and the clouds
some extraordinary kind of Neapolitan wrapped
in blood-stained bandages
the height of falling in acrostic menopower of pause
by that Grand Central of the interim
where we got up and slept
(everything) (according to)
(the gravedigger's) (tight) (schedule) as
that Friday morning literature opened up
an empty fridge
      on the lower east side of suicide
lip tonsured coercement
      an eye surprised that an i in melon matches
cloacal academies in part for
                                    the wish first

       was

                 then switches it

the wash

           fist

watching

            slugs

a deluxe in compensation for the snail-death

                  still imagined.

           You mean to say the unconscious is a lost

conscious

              not an unofficial sub-conscious?

That could have been me speaking a mirage
backwards to the possible
and happy times to be among those goodly hills
of incunabula

        mind meeting words
        in spatio claritas

                rough guess is

that's a genuine smile despite the poly-grip's
long quantity of frailty.

Still, musn't grumble
Die Weldt is Worte
in a poker game with genes as genres and
a three-point turn at the morgue.

Snowflake state on solid ground by stylus rendered
a random walk-shock terrifies for wetter miles
trawlers returning unmolested to retention
desert clarities in outcast runes

   so dense was ourselves in that comfort zone
triple amnesia with ice in a crowded cafeteria
hysteria from the headache speech is
            that cinema where laughter meets its cough

                        Universal City that I am
You are
                  classified.

                  (*To the tune of Raunchy Moll*)
            But there's never much fun at the vicarage and
            with love buttons under the crucifix
            transitory Venus vectors linked to
            severe cases of a nephew's Gen-X potency

            parenthetically:
            we are definitely not a family we're
            an art collection plus three kids and a dog
            and we know that to be urban is to be close
            to electricity & things

Market fountain hub suburb thumbprint moratorium
for chicken thickenings
writing this as an on/off platitude I bend a spoon
spitting sugar

              the bitten fingernails belong to Larry
a baby-boom adolescent masterpiece when wearing
his shoes   in the proper manure

              Relation of port to whale
                     dirt pentagram to stoppage allegro

                 and stripped by spring

        a lie growing litoral
              internet sink drama by
              Committee for Negative Salvation

"But I don't have your gift for constitutional analysis"

and what with "the compliments of the editor"
and all the other pebbles at Willendorf eating Thebes cake
aurignacian physiognomy inside
        a sealed lipogram's assinine mobility
to patch day stressed
              coz abarraunt
(definiendum here with signature diagonal to cognitive sediment
the pancreas pen keys finally retreating
           into punk patria bruising
closer
to the line drawn through widdershins to verticordine alpine
strictures
heliotropic subsequence part redeemer matte
indignities a chiselled cythera pandemic nighty nites

and p.s.

> there's no Father Christmas
> when speech gives good said.

Treatise II
(Out of Pastoral)

"I was thinking of the spring i borrowed"
both clock-part and season
        sectional coast caught in a crossage of phonetic
inattention
manufirmation before phoneme after-birth
   rippling vestibular the wrist
swirls into chough

krinty
     kralooway
         palapum vrimteh

then into wine before whinny
the ingredient of salmon paths masked
through the southern creeks
             grand cru at their sources
dried out into hawk tails and lizard prints
Minerva springs at Chac Mool plateau
       Olympic patterns on statistics.

Turns page.

To end of sentence.

Punctum.

Stella Maris)

"Does that astrological chart have a best before sticker on it?"

Mermaid apothecary: horse of Troy.
We were and we remain a simple people. Boorish a tad but
                                        quaintly nuncupative.
Our streams clear though ballywicked. Our lies conjoining
plain horse-sense with sophismata
                    we are tenuous but not
extreme
        when telling the sound of
the Findhorn's name.

Television remains our dictionary a telepathic trap for
our volitions stirred by the toll-free psychics
in their celestial dung of heliports on top of hospitals
topic to our petal veins across
                                the bagel of history.

Treatise III

Allegory can only be addressed from its higher order in theology. Aquinian allegoresis does not present a parataxis of polysemy but a narratized, hypotactic, and ultimately "progressivistic" encounter with multiple and radiant semes. So there.

Among the palm trees (six) along Vistas del Mar (seven)
the odor (eleven) of Belarusian anarchists (three) bemused
by chess.

"Sun-puke to starboard"

"have a nice cliche"

"the profanation in such"

"redemption . . . .

So

why not call consciousness a collapseable beach-chair
on a spot in Malibu

(it's not that thinking too collapses, but rather
that all thoughts are reactionary)

—VE

Kristeva (phenotext) Lukacs (social alienation) =
critique of modernity gets
"romantic anti-capitalism" sub-theme: separation

+VE

Barthes death of the author
free-play Derrida
Jauss reader-response gives
the poststructural
its dissipative
features.

A detail of bird left
to trigger altercation amortizes "trigger" to

exterior signage.

Early Lukacs says turn to page eight
Barthes replies that the corporate combines silence
with any book-length analyses of off-shore profiteering
Derrida adds it's because the read pencil fails to trigger
that the maximally saturated syntagms fail
to yield up quiddity in any satisfying
mode of tangibility
Lacan counters with: the workplace is still feasible in its media
light
structured as a language
(& here the "we" maintains

a combinatory caution
typically homosexual in its shy qualities of social display.
And at this sudden junction or departure
Jauss and Cixous at the same time claim that
hybrid autobiography's still mainstream

Derrida to Lukacs:

through arbitrary care you might be shown that ashtrays
are really sudden recollections of a neat smoke
                                in rows.

Excuse me.

I was actually addressing the 36 year old semiotician
of this next sentence.
Both words spelled inexact.   Vocabulary:
a pyramid way to call you a cab as this adult empire
comes fully bureaucratized—come to think of it—to call it
instrumental
actually sets the stage to push between
                                to having done this before
and what image lights the lyric out. It's all
                                theoretically personal
its dream the same as my dream in the camp
where it starts, or it started without
someone else in the place of epistemological prose.
            The stress is on lability, its lapping as talk through
            the traffic of lists—or aesthetics between the shaving
            mirror
            where the computer referred to as a notepad comes to be

a part-remembered song.

                                   Lyric is melting.

                    Song as sound, that is,
                    the question when
                    a man gets   an erection
                    does he
                    weigh more
                    as it turns
                    out
                    yes

                    is the answer
                    to
                    a different
                    question
                    pertaining to this city as
                    a montage effect colder than
                    the rock he never wanted
                    but more personal
                    than bad

Turns page

"I was with a sick friend when it happened."

The make-up
temporarily yours and mine on America's night of television
                    Snow White and her seven swans
                                   conjugate the lily pads
unspoken
cigarettes in a dwarf June Emmy
for Miss Understood.

Treatise IV
(Post-Ontology)

Let each self be a sentence comprising 6 (six) million words
with each word a minimum of 5000 (five thousand) syllables
and over 2 (two) 000000 (million) for the largest.

> a.k.a.
> d.n.a.
> palindrome +
> reversible conjunction.

But let's not get too technical.
Suffice to mention that a verb burns a hole in this page
and despite the bottled Bacchante poisonality perched
on a story about eleven different obituaries
and the tonic sol-fah in the library microscopes
the particularities' dominion remains as vague

> as Vegas

> and then it's Stendhal's turn:

"The eyes that will read this
are barely opening now
to the light."

Photism in a blink.

Or once upon a sound, in a far-off mouth (hardly
a novel deprivation—just
that habit of distinguishing "yours" from "not mine."

And what better way to multiply awareness
grimly granting that it's Plato's polis we're still in
than as lethargic poets turned philosophers.

Meanwhile:
via the sovereign law of the onomatapoeia
it's guacamole at the Cucaracha & parthogenesis by tears
in a movie starring Kenou Reeves
invisible gyrations gyrate invisible contour outlines
forming substitute imitations along
streets of system
plastic paper over the writing speaking
what it deletes   if it deletes
is what was thought
a retching in the mouth in

telligence   to get from

the anus   to the   ism in

a small step measured

"entity"

(energy times the clinamen into matter =

next page:

"Bouy thought a night a figure minds festival
chronic lessening to crack hole dumps sport's fizz if it can then
can't
commit it wrinkled rag on a careful window—gerunds
when the light goes off."

                         Where the light comes from

zoomorphic words leave cities enter books as obstacles
obsidian anti-tracks thrown obese, punctual and inexact . . . .

          "And around it" i said, meaning
maganese is not a saint
the frog-faced ego in its edict-similes . . .

"I've been here before"
                                             said

as you were saying

               going there.

Treatise V

                              Swamp lesions are my prime
location
for a cultural western colored Pacific if it moves
                    shoot it
audio-policy alert scans all fiber optic surfaces for
                    advanced art of the ultra-pulse
a laserscopic aura soon abducts your ex-pet to tax break killer feet
Talmud settles into breviary logistics
          expired sphincter dentata data
cosmic impotence known as retrogenesis
               negotiated cyclone apparatus inducing all those foam
pads
with their sodium errors matched to arcane coupons
          goulash to gulag   it's a commonplace distinction
               in this diner
not even bothered to have ever looked this way
               condition of direction   stable
predication to production   language
baulking not talking

Libretto for a pantomime?

                                                        Elsewhere:

"you should be glad that"   calls come from
down in the verb "allusion"

                              "brings
                    the pigeon to its perch.

But suppose it "reasoned" not "rained" today

marbling my temporary tattoo with a genuine solution to
another subject's contrapuntal hernia, that way
to imagine a world without golf

                    how would Wittgenstein put it?

347. Does a writer who suddenly notices the word "lettuce"
actually think he's eating one
in the letters BLT?

Syntagms are less chains than mists, the changing
atmosphere of meanings surrounding
the problem that things think.
                              Each day mortality lexicons
                                        a tin can a cat rolls
                              into avalanche pears   a cancelled cataclysm
                                                whatever duration wants
                              attention waits.

            To the tune of "Johnny I hardly knew you"
                                        carapace of Theodosia fold-in
chronotopes
                        looks by you if it should to
                  morbid panty ethics
                              "stand by to end"   laborious
copies
                        of deodorant concordance citadels
                        asceptic tangram shaft toil between pauses
                                          "what would have brought
                                          this

                  to interrogation"

Ophelia growth in readership allowing page a place as cloned
firmament
       "pink" "pain"
            if rule corresponds to panic why change it to
"picnic"
    elephant buffalo battalions
    remnants of interregnum tusk regimes
        swallowed late in the game
hardware sententia through suede navel Dante dots
progressive porn on board translation planned by chunks
back from a ludicrous earlier proposition
denied multifarious
combinant boas left uncoiled upon a think-along
Texas ranger under caliph colored chaps
heterotopian plans flunked by mild inner historicism
thinking the sodom-flag is pirated
fold craft into concordat dating polysemy bathroom bid
a Torah in Hell totalling
the entire eighth of a shifter's wedge.
Stripped reading to wagtails equals a man eating dogs
eating cats eating birds eating worms eating
men eating dogs eating cats

at this mental level we can name advance.

              "My Child:
        the antients

                                    tell us
how writing occupies a fault-line across the fingernails.
        (My fist is clenched [dear one] as I write this sideways
to assure you that complementary Purgatory passengers
might still arrive by Micklemass sneeze-weed.)

            "and a merry chiasmus to sandy claws

        "and pepper up in the hot zone debits to remember

"that time sprinkles dust on the dino eggs

                "and fogs up choice in the interactive coaching

"outside the neighborhood's a neverhood for crablice profits

"remedial yodelers apart some devils in detail

            "take the nutmeg to dial in for three credits

                    "now the poultry has flipped

"and the hi-fat burger shuts its book

                "we have lift off

TREATISE VI

I put some hills in Tennesee around a jar that isn't there
with cold mimesis everywhere

        the long day trickles into sunrise
nostalgia breaks a leg along someone else's Sputnik Strasse.

Possessed of the social demon here i come
        a baby as a burp in a vortex
and — if the self is a spray-paint traced across the social field.
and — the human being emerges as the polysyllable in a world
    of monosyllables.
        Then it's time now for
noun alert.   There is a glitch
   in the image-quote.

    But waiting for Godot's not as bad as remaining for Rousseau.
    (If you are a member of our rabbit reward club please identify
    yourself.)
    Time's still a one-way street in a small village called space
    and it's entropy flopping up each day
    a random sunrise out of classical conditions.
    But with Herodotus and Napoleon your paparazzi coaching staff
    there will be time for history again.
    Phallic franchise: pride drops else droops.
    From Blake to Balzac it's the same masculine descent
    to the bonsai garden
    where the final lumberjack perspires triumphantly
    from overwork

S.L.O.T. 148

Draw then the line against all independent minds
and with this winter i thee wed.

But before we start this interview let me warn you that
when i speak i grow smaller.

Thus entered the haiku as the mother of all prose
sounds at first inscribed
in the grotto of a glottis-cave
carved from the throat of one
at Altamira marking the phoneme's pictogram
ear osculum itching silence
into sneezing.

There you have it.
Quite easy, really, once you see there's
a hidden conjunction in the either/or.
Call it a crucifix, a ghost in the ilex
even an orange wind.

> blushing blood but butter broken (3.5)
> bidding blimps build breezy breeds (3.5)
> beauty big brown bench betoken (3.0)
> benzene bivalve berth brake bleeds (3.8)

alternatively:

PLEASURE — SEIZURE
plus-je   si-je

if / i;   not / i;   but / i

"frozen zen popeye zone puppy over river rover running Heraclitoris
hystery dharmaquiddity relax either if / i then not / i yet still / i
millennial Lucretian what if / i question / i sign / struck ur / gency
what if a ball or ring a bell duel in dual in dividual jewel noema
poematic polymer muscle / ings by buy sexual black sheep shop
sheet in delicate delible Tibetan dead of the book tric(k)tatus
taught us tortoise training raining anonymous jump-start at art
part good line them to florelegium mirage user tips cholesterol
bluest bluer blew a scream resembling paper cripples ideology and
night!"

plus / je   si / je

        Painful to say but,
in representation we are satisfied. Thought-velocity spells yes as
no
(propaganda of a light wave-packet emitted in a question of
"perhaps")
        This stalls all curvature
runs risk back to a wall
up against it inertia dreams
desire at play, but "simplified."[1]
So we're flying across the stutter again,
that eternal returning to a primordial soup of sound.[2]
Ghosts pass on the sacred chowder.

How do we explain all this?[3]

1. Spiral to the ideal body: lose 16 oz. in only six millennia money-back guarantee!
2. Time's getting shorter so let's call a cow a now!
3. Prosthetic dawns applicable to shapes (turned off).

Opposite Poems

> "Poems will never do."
> —*Paul Blackburn*

LET US NOT BE DETAINED HERE BY THE POSSIBLE RESEMBLANCE
OF WORDS TO LIVES. FOR THE DREAM IS OF A DEATH IN PLACE OF
EFFRACTION. OF A NATION ALWAYS DYING IN PAIRS.

"The fourth amendment meets the tenth commandment
across an over saturated band of superstitions.
Nothing falls where you expect it.
At this point shall the non-we speak
always a mile short of the epiphany
in the window, dear, down by Harry Potter's foot?"
Claude Civility through his monologue relation
as a man to its beast in a parrot patois
yet truant to this stammering
a corpse flying into an exquisite crow.

This is neo-liberalism on its final bar stool
beneath Saran-wrapped reservoirs of profit
you can smell it by its teeth when it decides to breathe
communard sparky speak agent of the *hors texte*
just before supper and discourse meet in geometry
as weather patterns form around the White House where
current politics operate in a perfect condition
of impossible politics
the gestalt Santa Claus remarking less a crisis than

the constitutional contradiction at the heart of any suburban
Easter.

[*Enter the pram bomb.*]

It's clear why one's individual safety can never be an inviolable
constitutional right
and rightly so,
for here,
in the sleek good looks of the new global literature
the confrontation of non-commodity socialism
and supply-side Capitalism
no longer obtains.
This is where sunsets are served every half hour while skiing
in a Utah of vintage vodka.
Instead of that I could have mentioned
the sadness of Sir Thomas More
back turned to camera the moment after his execution
reflecting on the technical uncertainty of silence.
The knight referred to is also a nun in an unknown limerick
by John Gower
and the truth of all of this is wired for profit
with independent research security guaranteed
by the offshore dealers.
Each language game is complemented
by every interlocutor's ability
to disregard the final sentence as it plunges down into
incomprehensible interrogation.
There's snow too beneath a crowd of yelling passengers
but what I could have pointed out was that to utilise
the straight-line method of systems analysis

will always prove insufficient to resource accumulation
no matter how many times you slice it.
An entropic pull obtains towards a more traditional recipe for
différends,
for instance, to cure the city of its pedestrians why not eliminate
the car?
Ours remains a luxury world of details
smoothed along a post-national axis of leisure-certainties
that never need reshaping.

Or else I could have mentioned
André Malraux's theory of the lyric
that being as an " 'I' without a Self"
still current in a system of mottoes offered up to memorabilia
in convenient chronological sequence,
cut off by a shadow cast by a huge façade
painted according to the system implicit
in Rimbaud's "Voyelles."

I truly apologize for the way I live my life in a Bombay suburb
is not a practical claim nor relevant to this particular method
of in-house brokerage. Shania Twain is in Rio de Janeiro
a week before this is being written.
I could have joined her there
but the impacts
from a fourth cluster bomb exposed
a different range of secretarial concerns.
At which point a colorful and assorted group of artists
professional samba dancers and intellectuals
are discovered in a shallow grave marked *Cuisine Régional.*
A glib clarity appears on silk when gaining access

only through precise but unknown coordinates.
For instance
by extracting color from a pygmy image
a smaller tattoo emerges on the left eye
and pertaining to a claret quango
the senior appointments officer
squats translucent through its nude lunettes.
All the victims were given vanilla ice cream
packed in my own country
but not in my own back yard.
The voice sends a fax to its missing neurons
"Go seek the latex in their language."

But this might not have happened then or ever
perhaps it's just an aversion to merely descriptive windows
at the back of newsreels' historical slippage.
Then again, what of the lecture about the table that greets
the dissertation on the floor?
The fun of research arrives at a lacerating cost
to undecided alternatives
it's lamp past six or a quarter to door
and the adumbration in the phrase
"the darkness and the death" gets bypassed.

Fragile OF the world not IN it.
Or else I could have pictured the scene
as a rush to more complex personae
the checkerboard withholding a barmaid's nictitating face
and beyond the *repoussoir*
Cannalone Sistine College extra ceiling sometimes
similar to that continuum of birds known as

seasonal prediction.

Even the Renaissance came to the cheerless conclusion
that the phoenix is merely a pigeon in heat
despite what the High Priest said. Kosovo
is in the first hole but what's in the others?
The sensorium dances in its house of cards
retaining "defense and security"
as its two best selling points for death.

So instead of eating or venture capitals the test rats
build a labyrinth out of their carrot rewards
and if it works
the news reports what the facts can't say.
In which case sit quietly in as many linguistic forms
as are available to you in this eddy of technological trajectories.
Easier said than done
when even the social performees are poking you into
paratactic radiation fields.

Defeat always improvises with defeat
I bet those cockroaches at Hiroshima knew that's a good one
as did the Spice Girls each time they read *Rasellas*
over and over to themselves. You see
there really is a Happy Valley out there
somewhere under the pan-hydraulic break-up
of the infant guardians
beyond the errors of culture named symphonies.
But don't believe all you hear. For instance
that "there's a war on but no enemy"
it must come back to haunt their President each night

S.L.O.T. 156

he dreams of ice-cream golf courses in Kandahar
and all the world class pros are over par
because of pipelines underneath the cause.

Even the New Sentence won't help you.
Sucking some baobob tree lollipopsicle
the new-born Buddha emerges as an ampersand
of his own after-birth or, as Thomas Hardy must have put it,
beyond the Casual's gate it had lost the blew, tell, so,
breaking to midnight in a loss at cards.
You see the thorn is moon in June expenses
and camaraderie's incarnadine
the color of defeat when saying
he did hear a voice call as if taunted by
third-world trampoline production costs.

In sports this all adds up to the quarter-back's readiness
for percept-analysis
his temporal conjunctions relaxing at half-time
into paroxysm.
What would love be without life?
inquires the synchronized swimming mirror
and will all the mud-routines be compensated
or most of them,
or at least a few of them,
sometimes,
in some different time zone
questioning the peanut about its own
specific dispossessions in the hungry
mouths of the allergic?
But all of this might be decades ago

before the black clock's verisimilitude dissolved
at the moment when,
psychoanalytically,
the King and Queen were dissolved
by durability
and broad theories of quantum emancipation.
Everybody knows that
syntactic regimes precipitate a plethora of outcomes
placed along an axis whose poles are adjacency
and independence.
Random thoughts emerge to disappear
and finally return as a screensaver
on a damaged lap-top in Baghdad.
At least the squirrel put it that way
adding " immanence used to be a style of life."
He was a fat man and therefore a good man.
I am itself says the door opening for Melville
textured into a different formula to generate
the marbled whale of becoming.
As for myself I'm the self that I'm enduring
across the lining of an individual understood
to be a consistent yet fragile multiplicity
and with my own blood the back-drop
to someone else's anemia.

And folks know that the list goes on
bargain buckwheat basements, snatch shrinkers,
complimentary hose comprehenders,
stability conifers for the deck,
unjust mothers' ratatouille recipes,
civility perfume extracts, demarcation

uniforms for slivovitz repairs,
Pandora chapters about ancient cameo co-ordinates,
genetic catatonia among tziganes
with typhus kept in amnesiac zone-blocks
behind each outsourced rhetorical question:
"Who put you there, what's your purpose,
is everything the same as God left it
before her lunch-break?"
And God replies:
I am sometimes a face but rarely in town these days
though city localities return me in the form of
mundane coupons of surprise.
Hullo, dead literature
that literature whose aim is of the form
"this literature" but actually
"I have lived despite living."

The history of a culture
is the history of ideas gone
to auction.

Everyone I know doubts that the voice is more than just
a radio triumph cascaded around without body.
Pseudo-victorious as a soul in a supermarket
it transcends its corporeal limitations, bypasses the check-out
yet still pays its bill at ideology's beckoning.
Lacan won't tell you a thing about the impact of form in time
or how every landfill before becoming a polis is
both a house and a mountain.

But it can't be obsolete when it's never new.

The way George Bush appeared as an arsenal
complete with an aura around it,
face gaunt between its past
published in a magazine before it speaks.
A thousand news reports can't repeat *that* echo
when we show the mechanism behind the effect
and the cuckoo clock starts its confession.

But perhaps it's a relief to be trapped in
the crazy lingerie of serial reproduction?
Standing firm not for the party
but the moment.
Take Jane Fonda for instance, notice *her* value size,
but for whom?
The sole *value* that Adam Smith could see in coal
was to keep a worker warm
but now all the Q-tips come frozen and shipped
from Labrador.
Yet still the body might announce itself in language
as the logical collapse of signs.
Or so some people say
but *their* rule of supper is no rule
especially if you start with
communicability in the form of Diogenes
or five-year guaranteed sponge efficacy
upon Palestinian body parts.
We only experience how meanings are made
by pulling language apart
but try explaining that to their mothers.
King-twitter to fisher-bone
are you recording me?

S.L.O.T. 160

If not let someone else be your commercial surrogate.
What needs developing is a sensitivity to that kind of chaos
children seek.

But then again, perhaps we abuse language this way
in order to construct those opportunities for getting lost
in the city on week-ends, a final catharsis
of Summer
yet the morning we left Liège
was different
arriving at the station to see the Orient Express
depart the same way we did
to the west.

I lived once in the thirteenth century of words
when it felt a little younger at fifty-five
and a little older to be six.

The bar closes an allegory on Japan compacted
in a towel of pure experience.
Mel, the Civic Nemesis returning tanned
from his winter skiing, citric and simian, smiling
at cameras not people.
Even when you trip over them
the homeless remain invisible
why don't they go back to their Aristotle
and get a part-time job selling philosophies,
or redesign those flying buttresses on old music halls
that always need repairing?
As a child I fell into the wrong symplegma
a Caribbean kitchenette in the axonometric

with its letter-box a church door to cathedrals.
At which point several minor poets in
footnotes jeer and point their fingers
at William James and the Book of Kells
and Hegel's fractal twin in the hermitage that Ahab
docked at
sleeping in the corporate analogy of scaled-down
profit graphs.

The speaking trees made Dodona Disneyland
and softer spoken than Gilgamesh
with leaves
on the branches of the social casement
windows half attentive to the illegitimation
of the One as All.
Then suddenly I thought of something else between
traditional cryptic pursuits
and unconventional definition:
Anne Murray was doing "Snowbird" as a kindergarten
sing-along
the kind of political insurrection
that even Don Cherry's Masonic handshake
can't achieve
all preferable to free-speech and sheep bleating
from the Bay of Pigs.

Blake knew that an intellectual thing
is produced by holding a raw onion beneath one eye
the crystalline covenant of consequence appearing
in a few seconds.
But matter changed and now nobody cries without

a shovel to remove the mess,
even the Great Lakes are guilty
of their own filth and myth, and yet
when things get worse people get better
that's why I'm here totally incapable of ordering
my own noodle soup via Shelley's ekphrasis on Mont Blanc

Meanwhile, back in the Hall of the equine satellites
more questions arise:
When is a prisoner political?
Where do terrorists sleep at night?
Why don't our victims burn quicker?
Who are those bastards in antithetical American
star-ship enterprises fixing
the world price of oil
as its filament membrane snaps?

Meaning as use: the last great mist of insufficiency
ineptitude contiguous to mud-speckled gander problems
mulched into pastoral libidinal Adornos.
There are no national Sapphos in this sector's
chapter on capacity.

[*The pram bomb explodes.*]

However,
in an attempt to track the chronology
of an unchained event-action path
"Laurie buys her Wheetabix"
via innate syntax leaf-splatter surrogate coordinates.
A real tree gets successfully reattached

to the wrong leaf upon a false branch
such that the sub-assemblies of word proximities
we call Massachusetts Ave. and Noam Chomsky
create a link-chain-fence-effect giving way
to cubicle culture proximities.

But perhaps the point is subjectivity.
Maybe I am I above all clouds that worm your bookmark
cleansing the celery of its gestuary language
a pure tube of reinforced design remarkable
as truth is for its inauthenticity.
Like painting the swell of
some Jackson Pollock Language group
in forethought, intricate as prose would have it
and syntax
the one-hundred headed poodle collared to live music
in the karaoke factories that cause
unseasonably average weather from Vegas to Rangoon

Maybe so, but I was still in 1994
with millions of others like me when
1998 suddenly happened.
Or did it?
Was it eventually the rest of my parallax sandwich?
It felt like New York had finally arrived three
months before the birth of man.
But what happens to everything that never happened?
I could have played and won at chess
with Marcel Duchamp
and that way given him the idea for the readymade.
Yet who would have preserved the visible marks

of these events?
But it could have been a different question
such as "meanwhile what *is* reality?"
From now on each time I wake up I want
a written guarantee that what I've just been through
is an authentic period of sleep.
The name of the traveler sounds real but muffled
a thought drips at this point
onto a cumquat advancing into Saturday's fruit salad.

Then again the question could equally have been
"who speaks in my act of listening?"
The answer's known to be the caesura
of a new subject.
Caught in the call of a call within
anechoic memories of data-blocks
and birth prints, William Wordsworth renames
the *Lyrical Ballads Writing Degree Zeno*.
Poetry drops you in a field
where there's no distinction between this and that.
Take, for instance, suddenness
in the writing of Bruce Andrews:
each word finds its place equidistant from
an unstable plane of judgment
but what if the parachute doesn't open in your descent
into the words of thinking things?
A little short of memory a plane hits a tower of glass
and shatters
the disappearance of America!
Think that in Spanish: origin never was and
only new myths can narrate that

so that in a gesture become gestalt
it will have named.

Birth by drowning
and the salt of the Pacific on your shoes
and from a singularity of shorelines the memory
of a sign of what's to come. The hand that writes this is dying
and perhaps already

"the work that I was born to do is done."*

* George Chapman's words
  on completing his translation
  of Homer.

Indoors again, and "oops"
"I" is a life in everything it plays.
Right now
it's scrabble concurrently hoping that its kids
will all grow up to be a life and with a world
to put it in.
Thirty-six years cold and caught in
a spiral of peacetime paper
when all of a sudden these words become
a suicidal pronoun
capturing a little night boundary
strange to the car transporting
the conspiracy of its passenger.

Thus prose arose
on the omelet side of the felicitous

the cheese & scallion backstage on
George Oppen's plane of lunch of wives*

*See the third poem from
Discrete Series.

remaining aphoristic in the check-out time
before sunrise in a western.
Here, the reader relaxes on a mountain-top
halting the progress of the mirror.

It begins where it ends.
The rotation of reptiles into the image
of a Führer, at which point
con-substantially yours becomes
the rat's turn to multiply.
Then again, in these times and places
the verdant lattice across a dismantled casement
might reveal itself to be a human limb.
It's the same intellectual detour
through some *paysage moralisé* and everywhere
the iconography gets modified.
Auschwitz and abattoir:
two events where all that survives survives
as the composite of what we are.

Meanwhile in the Shadow of
the Valley of Disneyland
theorists discuss a second phase in mortuary versatility:
a picture gallery phase of dying having given way

to classic sentimentalism felt
as a medley of moods.

Placed on some desk a note tells
a smile is being beaten
and there are lapses in an African colloquium
precipitated by the sound
not the meaning of the word
stupidity.

Carlos Williams contributed a well-motivated wheelbarrow
to the Atlantic's notion of a use for language
but in Alberti's theory of structural cohesion
and—polytypically yours—
with Cezanne's apples born
for baked children,
there's no equivalence of ocean to
a *commensuratio* with the human body.
Basement level language, attic level speech
and nihilism
in everything that breathes.

Even the Chinese performance artist in Berlin
gets caught amidst a dramaturgy between two points
challenging the avant-questioning
with answers proceeding from a de-authored rot.
But what if someone said
"whatever is beyond is here"
and everybody listened?
Collect your autobiographies along the fault lines

across the quincunx of the suburb sutures while I sings for its
body poetic
among the anchovies of anecdotes.
Have you ever noticed how imposing
Ottonian church construction can be
and ever wondered why?
It escapes all the cult classics with its bold axiality
and clear articulation
the nave with its groin vault and transverse ribs
looks a little bit like post-industrial decorum.
It feels as if you're in the vast interior of a sermon,
solid as a sonnet, the page held firm by
an animated wall of words
with polyfoil oculi between them.
But could you live or worship in it?
Who needs a tower on squinches at the crossing
flanked by turret stairs and literature
some luminous interior of folding chevrons?
Convert the building to its "message"
inside the supplement "house"
and *home* remains
the absence of a gap.

But then again it might be better to imagine
the settling of meaning at sea, high tide
on Easter morning in the question
what is a cathedral when
reflected in water?
And it could be worse
after all we're still free agents of differentiation
and the moon remains

mismatched to the mountain
a discretion of interlace in the polyphony
of a child's landscape.
The happiest traumas start in verbatim clarity.
For instance, imagine entering my edibles
as the penultimate plenum of a Tokyo mid-morning
with Foucault permanently lost among cannibal dahlias.

Admit it's all a teleology in tatters,
a chapter on capacity and you
beside me in the wilderness
the blue-haired boy
his head against the Manet asking
"an't please your Laziness to rise and dine
on brittle blossoms' little treats?"

It was 1936 I think,
I was dressed up as a post-impressionist among apple trees
in blossom,
                    high 55.
Pat had just returned amidst a prodigality
of preternatural attention
from a hypothetical description
of a seedy weekend in Orlando and become
my chance to be Moses or nothing.
We both welcomed that detergent supercession
as a paraphrase incendiary
and imagined the touch of leather glass inside
the troublesome tribunal of
that subjective precession called
"a relationship."

Such promissory articulations make
our complex allegory sensitive
to hemorrhoid flare-up
a heliotrope in two
non-symmetrical extensions
the deal base four for fun
up a human triumph
but smother *this* on your face each day
and you'll live forever
with insanity recollected in tranquility
as a middle ground between "bequest" and "parochial."

Two times one times two equals
one couple from Michigan's plan
to build their dream house with human chains around
a single bank account.
Elsewhere the Simpsons enter *antanaclasis*
in the core of a lawyer's logic
and all stay attuned consumerly
to the mass-marketing of happy consciousness.
Stability precepts govern this prison-house in its night
of hasty occupations (as Pound once quipped
in this country no one has the time
to do things quickly).

But perhaps that's not the case
and if rape beats arson
then what's so medieval about Bill Clinton?
A sea turns Gothic at the sight of nanotechnologists
splitting the hair of a proton
while, back in Surrealism

seventeen legless spiders attempt to make a web
against the garish background of powdered human teeth.
Elsewhere a messianic community
caught in anaphora becomes nullified
by the remaining workable squad cars
in Nevada and suddenly
there's a quarantine again
and it's cited by Sainte-Beuve:

        "How

lovely

      to be well

             and still wishing

to be better."

It takes a lot of courage to talk of tulips
here on the edge of
participatory democracy
where whisky culminates
a biophysics of tradition
just as Jack drops the bottle when it broke.
At this point Lewis Carroll might step up
to remind us that in our mechano mirage
the difference between sense and nonsense
is not always to be found
inside the spectral materiality of language
but in the rawness of the truth
of simply being there
an expert in specifics
yet fundamentally a hope
without a cause.

That said
thanks to autopoeisis and its listeners
it's Springtime in the univocity of being
speech without voice
as the thought of the one voice
listens in.

But perhaps things are more practical
maybe we're following Deleuze
reformulating the poetic line as the
constant emergence of
an
event-
surface?

Either way it doesn't solve the question
as to whether it's the pre-geopolitical
or the post-historical that we're facing.

Do we all circulate in these nice days
as the rotary effects of an abyss?
Time and again I wake up to a single question:
"What went on in God's mind
before she finally decided to be God?"
Was it something like quantum physics
or closer to pure relaxation?

Dignity is brutal,
quietly brushing up against the word
                    "difficult"
as some Stalinist pickpocket prior to

a predetermined aporia.
The virtue of high-strategy repudiations lies precisely in
the pleasure afforded by each unmovable cornerstone
in the imaginary unity of abstract, professional
rejection.
Happiness would be anguish if it wasn't
for spectacular leaps into untried praxis,
like putting Christianity on trial
during the Tour de France.

But perhaps poetry is the consciousness
of being wrong at the same time
as the neighbor's cat needs feeding.
At which point
communication stops before a letter from
a complex urban space of anonymity
addressed
                    to the one who didn't find it.
There's nothing much outside the window
in the street,
                    except the same
solitary taxi
with its inevitable aromas of melon,
                    nicotine
and childbirth.

It was during the darker decades of the Bush era
among the medium-brown style preparations
for yet *another* banal intervention that
the cinema was redefined
as a new lie in movement to rank

a close third behind politics
and endocrinal diagnostics.
And before we reached the graveyard
the color from the road required better spacing
to facilitate the unknown events of the new
foreign policy in order to saunter by
into mandatory military service.
And here the dead arrive
in pristine condition
attentive to this lyric moment,
greeting each dawn from their body bags.

There's something aloof yet subjunctive
about the seacoast
in such centuries of sentences
the sudden shipwrecks caught
in their own similes without the warming
emancipation of vernaculars.
But if I say "mandate"
and you respond with "syzygy"
then the corporate scandals *may* disappear.
Iraq is not, however, another town in 'Pataphysics
and yet always beyond the supermarket products
swapped on television.
Home Entertainment Centers in Texas
facilitate the perfect seam
between war and sports.

But equally, perhaps this is merely a pause in the panic,
a white flag and then a truce before
the trigonometry sets in and Hegel lines up

with the rest of the world
outside the planetarium to witness once more
the end of History.

Or perhaps I'm privy to Martin Luther King
inattentive in his Bible study class
in the anthrax capital of America.
It could be Christmas day in Fellujah and life
celebrated as collective-death
and perhaps some President is grinning
on a cracked screen explaining
his rationale for the diacritical marks
over free democratic elections
assuring us that they'll be improved acoustics
in the next campaign
and a new brand of duct tape
to assist the ones who want to see.

The guard conducting the interrogation admitted
that we have a *situation* and then went back
to his book. Words don't suffocate
like they used to, here
they change functions until spring arrives
once more and they emerge
from hibernation as marginalia
or ephemera.

Ever noticed how all those captured
never have shoes on?
It's here perhaps, that the after-shock
of some persistent anti-matter makes

our present week
a consequence of not caring.
There are always the numerous scenarios:
a child, fully equipped with hard-hat
and rocket-crayons
paints the walls of the Pentagon
in the color of neutron
at which point
and being subject to
Pan-Socratic interrogations
reversible comments interrupt an answer
in order to stress the semantic complications
in election rhetoric.
Like Edmund Burke it has a plan
and plans to plan another plan
in the picnic grounds of national debt
and panic inconsistencies.

Subject to fits of secretarial paranoia
two Denver office workers scream
"it's never perestroika for pedestrians"
yet their godless self-god remains intact
as a consequence of which a slave attempts
to enter History over his all-day breakfast
in a corporate office for instincts.

But then again, perhaps everything's mutating
into a strict relationship of poetry to horror.
Both battlefields appear correct today,
thanks no doubt to Arnold Ruge
if anybody's heard of him

taking the carcass out of Germany in a vain
if not a proud way.
Or perhaps we're both at the zoo
but it doesn't feel like the zoo,
more like the idea of a concept of animal
when suddenly
an unrepeatable yet portable event
consults a travel guide to discover the kitchen door
seems to have disappeared.
A pun will *always* shatter Philosophy if it occurs
at a joint international committee
on creepy etymology
and perhaps it does.
But right now there's a contradiction
in the complex reason why music became
wall-painting and up ahead
is Presidential blindness and protectionism.

After a homage paid
to the crib of the unknown baby
(secreted into Arlington Cemetery
by a middle-eastern nanny dressed in black
clutching Clausewitz's *On War* between her resumés)
a micro-waved Barbie Doll re-emerges as the latest
tadpole of genetic cloning.
Two days later a different baby intervenes
in the current debate on advanced wrinkle therapy
offering its body as an active ingredient in
a break-through exfoliate supplement.
Its pigment changes
as Parisian street lights flicker like a gift from grandma.

Q: How does sociology deal with such frontiers
of skin inflammation?
A: It reads the label first
then breaks out into the comfort zone.

[Here a landmine explodes.]

But perhaps there isn't a zone of comfort,
or anything else thanks
to the third law of thermodynamics
applied to organized crime
and maybe I'm simply Piranesi reappearing
as a speech balloon
above the body of a dog he terms
the secular, productive intensity of time.

I was warned before coming to earth
that poets are less hygienic than novelists
leading to shorter lives
and a corresponding
rapid rise to fame.
Take that fucking little cheat
Thomas Chatterton, for instance,
the golden boy of all the Romantics
after he'd offed himself on drugs.
But putting that aside perhaps poems do have
a patrician origin obdurate and obfuscating
any intellect attuned to narrative.
It is the emergence of language as excess
its luminous vibrations settle far beyond
biography and psychology

as a petal greets a tear in a sudden regeneration
of poetic cliché
and this life as it happened.
You see it all the time: the picturesque of the propositional
in the image of a hiccup between two infinities.

But maybe Paradise is exile in experiment
and it is ours (whoever we may be) as an
epoch culmination phase of a spatial moment
on its way to a monumental nothing
out of something; a whole step of traffic stopping to look
hating: Food, Representation
even Fun (so Essential to any Model of Modernity
and ours in that order of differential commands)
and post-nostalgia for a limit horizon
set on classicism.

But then again
maybe there's a basic problem to thinking
the fragility of its balloons suspended as clouds
above a character in action.
Counter-descriptive agents at Abu Graib
suggest the scotographic is a valid alternative
to sleep
a hooded writing on its way to blackness
in all its insignificant singularities
making terror for poetry the outside of language.

Yet maybe a bullet through the head of language
allows sound to survive.
But what of the new silence published elsewhere?

Maybe punching holes in fossils
might allow us one last
Summer escapade as forgotten colonists
neither bugs nor butterflies but poets
conceived as the inorganic limit of the possible.

Speculative preciosity of that kind
may lead to endless permutations
but does it?
What if suddenly
I'm proof-reading Pierre Jean Mariette's
unforgettable two volume treatise on engraved jelly
at the same time, due to archaeological prognosis,
a tsunami hits Paris via a different school of painting
and a cardiac arrest
(brought on in a Spanish-style alcove)
conveniently provides sufficient plot line
for another episode of Emergency Room?

The wild dog in the test tube gathers strictly
nasal impressions of its percepts, ad hoc,
in parallel harness to every gabardine sentiment.
Here, wisdom is placed by an ancient Shaman
carved in soapstone out of character anomalies
recorded in the lost Euphratic codex inched between
the India Accord of 1883.
One writes a check and signs it "Helsinki"
in a cursive hand while high in a corridor
the data trail confronts the Expos of an epoch.
It's lunch-time in the park
where the person known as

the Fourth Amendment
reconfigures the evening for a visitation.

[*The proposition advances, stopping only at*
  the famous zig-zag in the clause suspended
  in its disappearing shape.]

Here, all the snail people congregate
in corporate hordes
but threat diminishes with inoculation
and intravenous tributaries rush to higher ground
or inland safety watering
car bombs along the way
that reappear as flowers among polka dots.
In festoons of aphasia a gun shrinks into its concept
to the time between the manner it invents itself
before an audience of misanthropic scientists.

Those years of heavy industry
now recover in hospitals
or convalesce in a network of fugues
without windows.
Still intact
the precarious syntax of vertebrae
await repair teams to arrive
from Hungary on horseback
and through all of this
there are churn owls at night
on the chalky download
beneath the silence of Cy Twombly.

If mine is the dream of last night
continued on indoors
behind the negligent delight
of secondary vibrations
from the hop-kiln-clarity
of foliage entering
the Chinese Year of the Tooth
then accidence is sufficient to express the needs
of sports-starved fans in somewhere other than
the index to the Gardeners' Calendar or Kalendar as it was
previously named where it is listed (sometimes)
between "siskin" and "putrescence" about an inch
above the year that spoke to conversations on
the impossibility in Hasselquist's disquisition
on the same or similar
subject.

Trust your instincts.
Then it ended. A painting out of context
in a late symphony by Handel
cortex at apogee marking the function
of love in
a non-
constitutional alignment
trapping in a copper abreactor
all the infant connections:
"headlines" "feasibility" "self-sustenance"
brief life in that pram-bomb before detonation
outside of infra-red frequency alerts
that leave a cashier covered in
blood-spatter patterns clean across
the low price of her Easter eggs.

Philosophers encourage us to think
that it's Elsewhere itself that takes up all the vacant spaces
but it's easier to imagine Wisconsin
as a vast inflexion and Canada

a cold cedilla over a giant American A
It's called the Linguistic Turn
and theory does it more effectively than poetry
which is still lodged in those familiar epistemes
and regimens of the vernacular
consecrated by the New York School

and then there is the worship of silence
and the blank
and the few still listening to Babel.

But you know the joke:
a man steps out of hypostasis into a quantum seriality
with "togetherness" his only "other" interiority
stumbling towards the necessity of History
with Dada and community
the distant echoes of that intimacy named conflict.
Word and thought seize this silence
it is each of the weekends it has never been
in the same boutique of your choice where
"revolution is symbolic
or not at all"*

*Baudrillard

CODA

I bet you thought the river would appear
a little lower than it did. Too bad
there's no forbidding it.
How many meanings to that foreign foundling?

Even a cloud knows when to fasten
its safety belt.

About the Author

Steve McCaffery is the author of over 25 volumes of poetry and criticism, most recently *The Basho Variations* (Toronto: Book Thug). He lives and teaches in the Poetics Program at the University of Buffalo where he is David Gray Professor of Poetry and Letters.

Chax Press programs and publications are supported by donations from individuals and foundations, as well as from the Tucson Pima Arts Council and the Arizona Commission on the Arts, with funding from the State of Arizona and the National Endowment for the Arts.

Arizona
Commission
on the Arts

**NATIONAL
ENDOWMENT
FOR THE ARTS**